PAST LIFE MEMORIES

AS A

CONFEDERATE SOLDIER

by

James H. Kent

P.O. Box 754
Huntsville, AR 72740
WWW.OZARKMT.COM

Library of Congress Cataloging-in-Publication Data
Kent, James H., 1939-

"Past Life Memories as a Confederate Soldier" by James H. Kent
Past life memories recalled through dreams and hypnosis.
1. Reincarnation 2. American Civil War 3. Metaphysics
I. Kent, James H., 1939- II. Title

Library of Congress Catalog Card Number: 2002113051
ISBN: 1-886940-84-3

Cover Drawing: Wayne Alfano
Illustrations: Morris Docktor
Cover Design: Brian Grimmer - theGrafixGuy
Book set in: GeoSlab703MdBT & FuturaMdBT
Book Design: Jackie Garrison

Published By:

P.O. Box 754
Huntsville, AR 72740
WWW.OZARKMT.COM
Printed in the United States of America

ACKNOWLEDGMENTS

I wish to thank you people who have taken the time to listen to my dreams and who encouraged me to put these strange dream experiences in writing to share with others. They include my sister Barbara, and a special thanks to my pen pal from Salt Lake City, Utah, Kristin Burton. Her assistance with literary information and her search for information to assist in corroborating the necessary historical details for this book, as well as her encouragement to write about these dreams will always be appreciated.

I would also like to express my gratitude to another pen pal from Tucson, Arizona, Pamela Titone, whose research and encouragement were also very helpful.

Last but certainly not least is my most never ending gratitude for the man who really made this book possible, Dr. Hans Holzer. His generosity with his time and knowledge, as well as his persistence to push this amateur writer into putting this book together can only be described as the highlight of my life.

TABLE OF CONTENTS

Introduction

When I first heard of James Kent's visions and psychic impressions, I was fascinated, not because of the subject, with which I have been familiar for many years, but by the way Mr. Kent went about corroborating the accounts of a previous lifetime.

His serious scholarship and careful, cautious approach have totally convinced me that this is truly an account of an earlier life and one more proof of the reality of reincarnation.

Not everybody is capable of recalling memories of prior lifetimes by any means. But whenever there is some unfinished business, or some information that needs to be corrected for the sake of the historical record, such events seem to occur.

Regressive hypnosis as a tool following up on dream material, especially recurrent dreams, is then able to widen the horizon and obtain additional details.

I discourage hypnosis to search for reincarnation evidence. There needs to be deja vu experiences, memories of events not of this lifetime, and compelling feelings that one has been in other places and times, which then need to be researched.

Naturally, any knowledge of such places or events by the subject must be absent, to accept the authenticity of the information.

Mr. Kent's case is an excellent example of spontaneous, recurring memories not of this life, and his research is wholly professional.

I am only too happy to say that at last a good publisher has agreed with me that Mr. Kent's book deserves all the attention and respect it will undoubtedly receive.

Professor Hans Holzer, Ph. D.
Parapsychologist, author of
LIFE BEYOND, BORN AGAIN, and BEYOND THIS LIFE

Introduction

CHAPTER I

REINCARNATION

Can you remember your past life? The very thought of remembering where you were and what you were doing 100 years ago, or perhaps 200 or even 1000 years ago is a subject that is both controversial and fascinating. Although there are many religions throughout the world that accept reincarnation as a way of life, many people have doubts that such a possibility could ever exist.

In the past 20 years there have been numerous books published on this subject and many dealt with the use of hypnosis as a method of liberating the dormant secrets of a past life. Many subjects of hypnosis were able to attain such a deep state of relaxation, they were able to temporarily put their present life aside and visit a previous life they never knew existed. They became aware of such personal details such as their name and place of birth and occupation in that lifetime. Even their surroundings were vividly clear to the point they could describe everything around them. Although most of the subjects of hypnosis I have read about were of an obscure mundane existence, quite often the information given by them could be verified through research of old records in the town where he or she was alleged to be born.

My first awareness of reincarnation began when I read of a housewife who became a subject of hypnosis at a party. Mrs. Virginia Tighe of Pueblo, Colorado was hypnotically regressed to a previous life in nineteenth century Ireland. This hypnosis took place on November 29, 1952 by Morey Bernstein. While under hypnosis, she talked in an Irish brogue of her life in Cork, Ireland, where she said she was born in 1798. She said her name was Bridget Kathleen Murphy, who was nicknamed Bridey Murphy. Although Mrs. Tighe had no current knowledge of Ireland's history or language, she gave vivid details of her life there, including the memory of her death at the age of 66. When the book *Search for Bridey Murphy* by Morey Berstein was published in 1956, it created a sensation. I tried to keep abreast of the news of this hypnotic event and from what I read as the years went by, a great deal of verifiable facts surfaced from the investigation of the life of Bridey Murphy.

Of the numerous articles written in many parapsychology books about reincarnation, the most common occurrence seems to appear in the Islamic nations, where there is nothing strange about remembering your past life, as this is their religious belief. On several occasions I have read of young children in Islamic nations having vivid memories of their past lives. One young boy I recall reading about had memories of being married with children and owning a business in the next town, all of which occurred many years before he was born. His intimate knowledge of business partners and family members of that previous lifetime has verified his previous existence to the satisfaction of everyone concerned. Many of the people of these nations have such previous life memories without the necessity of hypnosis.

My interest in parapsychology has led me to become an avid reader of various books on the subject, including several books by Dr. Hans Holzer, who at this writing, has written 120 books on various subjects of this nature. I have also been a subscriber to Fate Magazine for almost 40 years, which also deals with a variety of interesting and unusual experiences.

My first experience with reincarnation came to me about 24 years ago when I dreamed I was a sergeant in the Confederate Army. Since I had no interest in Civil War history, I thought this was a very unusual experience indeed. My knowledge of the Civil War was about third grade elementary school level at best. I knew it was a war between the North and the South, and it was fought from 1861 to 1865. 1 was never sure of the actual cause of the war, although I assumed slavery was a main issue. The dramatic portrayal of the Civil War in the movies and on TV were of more entertainment value rather than educational to me.

I knew the North won the war, of course, but the places of battle were completely foreign to me. Towns such as Antietam, Manassas, Spotsylvania and Chickamauga were not only unheard of in my knowledge of geography, I couldn't even guess in which states they were located. If you ever noticed, historians will speak of the battle of Shiloh, for example, but they never mention the state. They assume everyone knows it's in Tennessee.

As for the uniforms. I knew the North wore blue and the South wore gray (or so I thought). I knew that General Lee was the commander of the Army of the South and General Grant was the commander of the Army of the North. I would have been hard pressed to name any other generals, even as recently as a few years ago. Whenever I heard another General's name, I never knew if he fought for the North or the South, and if a General's name came up in conversation with a Civil War buff, I didn't dare ask.

It is unusual, but I don't remember anything being mentioned in our history classes in school about the Civil War. For an event of such magnitude to occur in our own country and not teach it in school seems like a major oversight. It seemed that our studies of that period in history were more confined to the life of Abraham Lincoln and his eventual presidency that carried the burden of the Civil War. Our attention was more focused on the early life of this man who would one day be in the awesome responsible position of making decisions daily that would determine the life or death of thousands of young American men.

Since most of American history was taught in the elementary schools, we learned he was born in a log cabin and worked as a rail splitter and educated himself by hours of reading. As he matured and became more educated he became a lawyer and later ran for President of the United States. He was elected, and assassinated at the beginning of his second term, less than a week after Lee's surrender. Of course, we also learned and even had to memorize his famous Gettysburg address, even though I'm sure most of us at that age had no concept of its meaning. We were taught that President Lincoln served his whole term as President during the war between the states, but we never actually learned what the war was all about.

I don't know why I never became interested in Civil War history. I guess I found it confusing or possibly even a little boring. I just didn't seem to understand what the whole conflict was about and never really had the desire to go to the library and learn something about it on my own. It has only been in the past few years that a re-enactment of the Civil War has become an annual event at one of the local parks. The re-enactment consisted of camps of both armies with their tents pitched at two separate locations on the park grounds. The re-enactors were careful to wear and use only authentic uniforms and equipment of that time period. Visitors were welcome to visit the campsites and ask questions of the re-enactors, and also attend two mock battles that usually took place in the late morning and early afternoon. My first time at this event gave me the impression that many of the visitors were really knowledgeable about Civil War history, especially from the conversations I heard all around me during the battle re-enactments. As I visited the camps I found that I was getting emotionally sentimental as I entered the Confederate camp, a feeling I had not felt when I had visited the Union camp. It was a wave of sad emotion that came over me, a feeling for which I had no explanation. While my visit to the Civil War re-enactment was interesting, I still hadn't a clue as to what the scheduled mock battles were all about or where they originally took place. After all, the battles of Little Round Top or Bloody Angle meant nothing to me, and I didn't dare ask anyone who actually won the battle.

I don't know whether it was just the school system 1 attended that omitted Civil War history from its lessons or if this is common in schools nationwide. Perhaps we may have touched upon the subject briefly with a few significant names and dates that I don't recall, but surely nothing in detail. The details of this dream and the ones that followed are so vivid and unforgettable that I have been advised to write about them. Some of the activities that occurred and some of the situations I found myself in may seem unusual, but I'm sure not everything that ever occurred on a battlefield was recorded in history books.

The controversy about reincarnation has frequently been written about in tabloids. One popular tabloid has written about a claim by archeologists that they have found ancient texts that made numerous references to reincarnation. I have read in several newspapers and magazine articles that reincarnation was often omitted in the Old Testament in order to instill fear of the eternal damnation of hell in people. The theory behind this omission of any reference to being reborn in a new life was to make people fear the consequences of death to a point where they would try to live a life free of crime and sin.

This same tabloid also featured an article on the belief of reincarnation of several celebrities, one of which was Glenn Ford. While under hypnosis in 1978, he was able to recall a past life as a cowboy in the 1800's. He said he was shot and killed by rustlers. The names he mentioned while under hypnosis were later researched and it was discovered that these people actually lived in the time and place mentioned by Glenn Ford while he was under hypnosis. According to this same news article, Mr. Ford had another hypnotic experience that indicated a former life as a piano teacher in Scotland in the early 1800's. He proceeded to play the piano even though he had never had a lesson. His name in this past life was given as Charles Stuart. When researchers went to Scotland to verify his identity of such a person, they found his grave and learned he had died in the 1840's.

Although the die hard skeptics may emphatically refuse to consider such a possibility of the human soul experiencing many lifetimes, I read in a recent survey that over 25% of the people in the United States do believe they have been here before. I don't know if all of these people who consist of the 25% have had a personal experience of remembering a past life, or if most of them are just open minded to the possibility. When you consider the numerous religious denominations and their different beliefs and methods of worship throughout the entire world, can we honestly make an accurate determination of which religious practice is the correct one? We can only determine what is the best or only acceptable method of worship for ourselves.

Since the dreams I have experienced were not only vivid and unforgettable but a learning experience as well, I have decided to write about them. Perhaps by sharing these unusual dream experiences with others, many will find their thinking a little more flexible and perhaps a little more tolerant.

CHAPTER II

MY PSYCHIC AWAKENING

In this present lifetime, I was born the youngest of three siblings in 1939 to a poor family in Trenton, N.J. I always remembered my father being in poor health, and his lack of a complete formal education led him to some of the most laborious factory jobs at minimum pay. His health soon deteriorated to a point were we had to survive on government assistance.

My sister, being the oldest, married her childhood school sweetheart and moved out to start her own family. As my brother and I finished high school, we both accepted low wage manual jobs. Soon, we both acquired employment at the U. S. Postal Service where we each worked for 35 years before retiring. We cared for our parents when we graduated High School and continued to care for them until both passed on in the late 1970's. Neither my brother nor I have ever married and we continue to live in the same house we bought to share with our parents over 40 years ago in 1959.

I first became interested in parapsychology when I was in my 20's, because it seems that is when I started having strange experiences with prophetic thoughts and dreams. I even had a prophetic vision while walking to my car one night. I had just left work at 11:00 PM on a summer night in 1963 and was walking down the dark deserted street to my car when a large "projector screen" appeared before me. I could see my hands on the steering wheel of my car while driving my usual route home. I could then see a bus stopped at an intersection ahead of me on my left. As I approached the intersection, a car suddenly darted out past the bus and into my path. I slammed on the brakes as hard as I could, and my car started swerving side to side as if I were on ice. I was heading right for the side of the car when the vision ended. The whole scenario probably lasted only a few minutes , but it left me badly shaken. I stood there trembling on that dark deserted street. I was amazed and confused at what just took place. I thought this must be an omen, so I vowed to be extra cautious on my way home that night.

As I drove along that familiar road, I could see that intersection ahead of me. I was driving slower now just in case, as I was still nervous from that vision experience. Sure enough, a bus pulled up and stopped at the intersection. I still thought it was safe, since I was driving more slowly now and I didn't see any other car. As I approached the intersection, a car came out of nowhere and darted past the bus into my path. Just as in my "vision" I slammed on the brakes and my car went sliding side to side. That car barely escaped a side collision as I continued to drive through the intersection. If a traffic light had existed there at that time, there would have been no problem. A brake inspection later revealed a little oily substance on my brake shoes.

Would I have hit that car had I not been driving more slowly due to the warning from that vision, or was it destined to happen the way I saw it anyway? That's the only time I ever had a vision and it may have saved my life.

Other similar strange incidents that occurred mostly in my early to mid 20's caused me to be interested in the paranormal. A dream I had in November 1960 of the death of a famous actor was the subject of an article I wrote for Fate Magazine. It appeared in the August 1999 issue, and after 40 years, that dream occasionally replays in my mind. The details were too strange to be only a coincidence.

****

FRANKLY, MY DEAR ...

I heard on the TV news one evening in November 1960 that Clark Gable had suffered a heart attack. I heard another report later that evening that he was resting comfortably and was expected to recover.

I took this news with some interest but little concern. I had never been a fan of his nor of any other actors of the time, for that matter. I just wasn't a big movie buff. I went to bed with no thought of the news.

That night, I dreamt I was standing at the end of a dark hallway filled with white smoke or fog. In front of me was a white-walled foyer bathed in a bright light. Suddenly, Clark Gable stood facing me with a big grin on his face. He was about six feet tall and appeared physically trim. He stood before me in a white shirt with sleeves rolled up to his biceps, his clenched fists resting on his hips in mock defiance. He appeared to be only about 28 years old.

I didn't say a word as Gable rambled on and on about how much he loved his movie career, and emphasized how important it is to be in good physical shape to make movies. He seemed jubilant. Suddenly, he stopped talking and became somber. He shook my hand and said, "Well, I have to go now." With that, he turned to a white door on his right and opened it.

Startled, I heard a woman's panicked cry on my right. "No-o-o-o!" she hysterically shouted. Mr. Gable paid no mind to the woman and quietly closed the door behind him. The woman rushed in front of me and tried frantically to open the door, but to no avail. She was middle-aged, about 5 feet 5 inches tall, with a stocky build and short, wavy blond hair. She wore a red dress and large pearls around her neck. As she pulled on the doorknob, her frustration flowed into tears. She turned to me with her head down and threw her arms around my neck, sobbing uncontrollably. I didn't know what to do or say, so I just patted her on the back. Then I woke up.

The next morning, the dream was fresh in my mind. I wondered who the grief-stricken woman was. She was not a young, beautiful starlet, as one would expect to find keeping company with a famous, dashing actor. I was shocked to learn on the morning news that Clark Gable had died that night.

The dream stayed in my memory long after that night, but the real shock was yet to come. Five months later, I passed a newsstand where the new issue of *Life* magazine had just arrived. I froze with goose bumps. There on the cover was a woman with short, blond, wavy hair and pearls. It was the woman from my dream. On her lap she held her baby son, whose father had passed away before he was born. She was Clark Gable's widow Kay Spreckles.

****

Another incident that was somewhat prophetic occurred in 1963. It was November 21 and all afternoon and evening I couldn't shake a depressing feeling of gloom and doom. I was at work but I had no reason to feel this way. No one close to me had passed on or was ill, and I always experienced a feeling of camaraderie with my fellow workers. Premier Kruschev was always "rattling his sabers" and making threats, so all I could think was that Russia would probably start a nuclear war with us. I just knew for certain that something catastrophic was going to happen with worldwide consequences, but I couldn't pinpoint what it would be. The next afternoon while preparing to go to work, I heard on the radio that President John F. Kennedy was shot. Now I knew why I had that ominous feeling of impending doom.

Some of my other family members have had their turns at experiences with the paranormal. While my brother and I were growing up we shared a bedroom in a little cramped apartment in the business district of Trenton, N.J. It was the summer of 1953 and the Korean conflict was just coming to a close. As we slept soundly one night, I was abruptly awakened by my brother's shouting. Suddenly, from a position lying flat on his back, he bolted upright and was shouting in what sounded like a oriental language. I lay there looking at him in disbelief. First of all, he was always very soft spoken, and I knew he wouldn't be able to talk so loudly. I also knew he has never learned or been exposed to for any length of time, another language, especially an oriental tongue. It also seemed physically impossible to wake from a sound sleep and bolt upright to a sitting position with your back so straight. His shouting must have lasted only a few minutes, and he fell flat on his back still sound asleep.

At first I thought I must be dreaming. It's a wonder his yelling didn't wake our parents or other apartment residents for that matter. As I looked at the alarm clock on the nightstand, I got an idea. I grabbed the clock and turned it around so it was facing the wall. I knew that once I fell asleep I wouldn't know if this was all just a dream unless I did something.

Sure enough, as I awoke the next morning, the alarm clock was facing the wall. I had confirmation that what I witnessed last night actually occurred. I told my brother about his nocturnal behavior the next morning. He didn't remember a thing that night, and he thought it was strange, and a little funny. I could tell he didn't know whether to believe me or not, but I think that when I told him about the trick with the clock, he was convinced.

I don't know if reincarnation was playing a role in his behavior that night, or even if the Korean conflict somehow played a clairvoyant or spiritual possession role. We had no relatives in the conflict that we were aware of at that time, and the war did not seem to generate the interest and concern among the American people as it had in World War II. It seemed as if a dying Chinese or Korean soldier was shouting his last command while his traversed spirit was using my brother's body as a receiving vehicle.

I believe now it is possible he may have experienced an episode in his past life in the orient. I always wished I had a tape recorder handy that night to record his foreign ramblings. I would have asked the assistance of someone who is knowledgeable in that oriental language for an interpretation. It may have even been an ancient language. I was witness to a very strange event that night, which I don't believe has ever happened again.

Our whole family was raised Catholic, so I'm not sure whether other family members believe in reincarnation. However, it seems most of us had some experience with psychic phenomena at one time or another. My mother had displayed a psychic gift on occasion and my sister has had prophetic dreams. One incident that occurred in 1956 is a good example. My mother had fallen asleep on the living room chair one early evening while watching TV. My father had gone to bed later that evening. Several hours later, my mother had a dream of my father's mother, who had passed away in 1953. In the dream she was repeatedly telling her, "Check on Harry!" "Check on Harry!" My mother awoke and immediately walked into the bedroom. A lit cigarette was smoldering on the pillow next to my father's face. Apparently, my father had fallen asleep while he was still smoking. Grandma was still watching over her son.

My sister's psychic dreams usually dealt with a prophetic or clairvoyant knowledge of a death in the family. For example, she told me she had a dream back in 1984 of walking into a funeral parlor and seeing the name of Joseph Kent on the doorway. The next day, she read in the obituary that our uncle Joe Kent had passed away. We hadn't heard from him or anything about him for years.

Another dream she told me about occurred in 1968. She had a dream that our cousin Dolores, who had passed away several years earlier, told her "Lisa is with me." As far as we knew, there was no Lisa in our family. Months later, she was talking to Dolores' sister and told her of the dream. She told my sister that Dolores' daughter had gotten married after her mother's death and eventually had a premature baby girl who died shortly after her birth. The baby's name was Lisa!

My father never mentioned any dream experiences of a psychic nature or any strange occurrences that seemed to be more than just coincidence. I don't recall my brother ever relating a paranormal event to me, although I was a witness to his strange behavior that night in 1953. Aside from these strange cases of the paranormal, I don't believe any of my family members has had a past life dream. I asked them on several occasions if they ever dreamt of looking entirely different and living in a different time in the past. The answer was always negative.

When I first saw an ad for a subscription to Fate Magazine in 1965, it seemed like a publication that would definitely capture my interest. It was from reading many of the fascinating articles that I became familiar with some of the contributing authors and their work. One of these authors was Hans Holzer. His occasional magazine articles led me to read his books. To this day, I never cease to be spellbound from reading of his exploits in contacting the restless spirit of the deceased, to identifying someone's past lives through hypnosis. I never would have imagined that a series of future events would one day bring us together for a session of hypnosis. As you will see in the following chapters, a whole new experience in exploring my past life awaited me.

CHAPTER III

THE SKIRMISH

My first dream of the Civil War occurred in October of 1978 and found me walking across a field with a small group of men. It must have been in the middle of summer since the sky was so blue and clear, but the heat and humidity were unbearably brutal. Our destination for the moment was the woods that stood a short distance before us. Not only would it offer shade from the hot sun, but also would provide sanctuary from the approaching Federal troops who have been relentlessly pursuing us.

Although I knew I was a Confederate sergeant in charge of the platoon, it was apparent none of us were actually wearing uniforms. The men consisted of a variety of sizes, shapes and ages, but all were wearing pants and shirts of civilian attire, and each one had a knapsack or other light basic gear as well as their rifle. I don't recall the type of trousers I was wearing, but I remember my white shirt with the baggy long sleeves had a silky feel to it and was sticking to my back and chest from the extreme heat and humidity. I was also aware of my straight black hair being matted down from the sweat.

We knew we had to keep moving, as the Federal troops were only maybe a half hour behind us. For the moment it seemed that the weather was our worst enemy, but I thought as soon as we were in the woods perhaps we could find a shady cooler place to rest. The men didn't talk much even though we stayed only about 8 feet apart. It was obvious we all were very much in need of rest.

When I experienced my first dream of the Civil War, I was about 39 years of age. I am 5'9" tall, and my weight is usually around 170 pounds. As the platoon sergeant in my dreams, I am about 23 years of age and well over 6 feet tall. My stature is lean, as would be expected of a soldier eating on the run.

As we approached an opening in the woods, I noticed a rut in the dry caked dirt, perhaps made from a cannon wheel when the ground was soft and wet. I remember looking down as I walked so that I wouldn't twist my ankle in the rut. I also remember seeing my rifle in my left hand, and my leather cartridge pouch dangling at my right side. The pouch was about the size of a woman's purse, and made of soft dark brown and black leather. It was supported by a wide leather strap that hung across my chest and over my left shoulder.

As we entered the woods I could feel some relief from the hot blazing sun, but the thick underbrush became our newest obstacle. The men struggled to find their footing for the first 20 feet or so, and the tangled underbrush soon gave way to a more clear ground with less obstacles for walking. While we tried to stay as close together as the rough terrain would allow, one soldier seemed to stay by my side. He had light brown hair that was thick and well groomed, which was unusual considering the hot humid weather, as well as our circumstances. He was almost as tall as I, and perhaps a few years younger. He didn't seem to be bothered by the heat as much as I was, and we talked and even laughed a little as we started to trudge through the woods. I felt more of a close friendship with him than with the other men.

Suddenly, I heard a barrage of artillery fire coming

from the field behind and to the left of us. The Federal troops had caught up with us sooner than I expected, and since we were so outnumbered the only sensible thing to do was to run. As we started to run through the woods, I could see ahead about 50 feet on my right what I thought to be a ditch. I didn't think we could run very far in the woods before we would be caught, so I hollered out to the men to run for that shallow ditch and lie flat. I had this desperate idea that if we lay flat as we could and kept quiet, the pursuing Federal troops might just not see us and keep running right past us.

One thing that clearly stood out in my dream was a large reddish-brown tree next to the ditch. It had a rough bark, and a large root of that tree was protruding from the ground. It appeared as if the whole length of the top of that root was sheared off, perhaps by lightning or artillery fire, exposing a beautiful red grain.

While it seemed we had all made it to the ditch, I heard a gunshot and a yell. As I peered over the edge of the ditch, I saw one of my men falling face down about 50 feet from the ditch. He apparently was too far from the ditch, and I assumed he caught a stray bullet from the Federal troops who were still coming across the field. My first thought, I am ashamed to say, was that he would give our hiding place away. If the Federal troops stopped long enough to attend to their new prisoner they would probably see us. This ditch was only an act of desperation that might work if the Federal troops didn't have to stop for anything.

About 20 feet beyond the wounded man were thick bushes and scattered trees, as was most of the terrain around us. My only thought was to get the injured man back to the ditch to see how badly he was wounded, and to keep him out of sight of the approaching Federal troops. I knew I could probably run the distance to where he was lying, pick him up and run back to the ditch in less than a minute. Presuming the Federal troops were still a safe distance away from us, I put down my rifle and leather cartridge pouch and ran over to the wounded man.

I could see that he was unconscious and his right thigh was soaked with blood. He was a stocky built man in his 30's. He had balding light reddish brown hair and a short beard and mustache. He was wearing boots, tan breeches, a white shirt and a vest. The thought crossed my mind that I may not be able to lift him due to his stocky stature, and even though I was very tall, I was also very lean. As I braced myself to try to lift him, a Federal trooper stood up from behind a large bush about 20 feet from me and aimed his rifle at my face. I was shocked because I didn't know they had gotten that far and were already in the woods.

I froze for a few seconds and then made an attempt to pick up my wounded comrade. As I started to bend down to pick him up, the Federal trooper raised his right elbow to squeeze the trigger. I again stood up and froze. We went through this gesture several times without saying a word, and I wondered what he was waiting for. Why didn't he shoot? All I could think of at this point was that he probably wanted to shoot me right between the eyes, and at this close range he couldn't miss. It also went through my mind that I could probably be dead before I hit the ground. I knew that once he fired his rifle, he would have to re-load, and by luck if he missed me, I just might have enough time to pick up my wounded comrade and run for the ditch.

As we stood there looking at each other, I realized how disciplined this Federal trooper must be. It was so unbearably hot, and yet he wore his hat and jacket, which appeared to be buttoned up to his chin, although I could not be sure of that because he sported a large black beard. I guess he didn't like the idea of shooting an

"As I started to bend down to pick up my wounded comrade, the Federal trooper raised his right elbow to squeeze the trigger."

unarmed man who was trying to help a wounded comrade. I was shocked and totally surprised when he quickly raised the barrel of his rifle and fired over my head. He cursed out loud as I quickly lifted the wounded man over my shoulder and ran as fast as I could while carrying such a heavy load.

As I lumbered down the shallow ditch and carefully lay the unconscious man down, I told the other men about my close encounter with the Federal trooper, and how he could have shot me right between the eyes, but chose to spare my life. I believe he cursed out loud so that his fellow troops would think he missed me because of a bad aim, not because he felt a moment of compassion.

Neither my men nor I had any heart to shoot to kill after that Federal trooper spared my life. As we fired our rifles toward the field where the pursuing Federal troops were coming, we kept our aim high. The fire was returned by the Federal troops which also seemed high, as pieces of bark from that tree next to the ditch flew off from the enemy bullets way above our heads. I don't know how my men and I assumed that, due to a personal encounter between myself and a Federal trooper, both sides would suddenly acknowledge a desire to shoot over the heads of each other and go on our way. In retrospect, it was very foolish of me to assume the return enemy fire, whose rifle shots were high and off the mark, were in fact anything but random firing from a distance or a poor aim.

There was no communication between us and the Federal troops, and our good intentional mercy shooting was probably not even acknowledged as such. My men became careless, as I recall my tall friend standing up from the ditch, and with one foot resting on the edge of the ditch, he started shooting toward the field, obviously keeping his aim very high. The only thing he could have hit at the angle he held his rifle would be a flying bird.

Quickly, the Federal troops fanned out in the woods, as we continued to shoot over their heads. I even remember one Federal trooper trying to take cover behind a double trunk birch tree, which left him quite exposed. I turned around to check on my comrade with the bloody leg. I was staring at his face and chest to see if he was still breathing and I woke up.

This dream has been in my thoughts all these years, but it wasn't until I decided to write about these reincarnation dreams that I decided to do some research to see if I could find any information relating to my dream. I found it interesting that my reading indicated that the battle I was fighting in the woods may have occurred prior to August of 1863, because that is when the repeating rifle was invented and first tested by Abraham Lincoln for the Union Army. In my thoughts during the dream, the existence of a repeating rifle never occurred to me.

Upon my awakening, I thought it was very unusual that we were fighting without uniforms. I learned that this was not unusual for the Confederates. Confederates without uniforms were especially common in General Lee's Army of Northern Virginia in the early years of the Civil War. By 1863, however, uniforms were more available for distribution among those same troops. I also thought it was strange that the Federal trooper who spared my life was wearing a black uniform. I thought they all wore blue. At least what I could see of his uniform was black. Since he was standing behind a thick bush, I couldn't see his trousers, but his jacket and hat were black. While browsing through a book that illustrated Federal uniforms, I found that black uniforms were worn among the New Jersey, New York and Massachusetts regiments.

This dream was in such vivid color that I remember

the ditch we were trying to hide in was actually clay, not dirt. I believe it may have been only a natural downslope of the ground, rather than a previously dug ditch. As I pressed my hands against the clay while trying to crouch down as much as possible, the clay felt cool to the touch, even though that day was almost too hot to endure. With my face so close to the ground, I remember the clay was a reddish-brown and gray mixture. It's still a mystery to me what caused that big tree root to become shaved off at the top, exposing that beautiful red grain. Perhaps that part of the woods had been the scene of a long battle before we arrived, and the tree root was grazed by artillery.

I still find it hard to accept that we were trapped in that ditch by overwhelming numbers of Federal troops, and we didn't have the heart to kill them because my life was spared. The Federal trooper who had his rifle aimed at my face was a big husky man who appeared to be about 40 years of age. Perhaps he was a career army man who may have been close to a pension but was caught up in the war like the rest of us. His large black beard was unique in that it wasn't just long, it was full and even a little wavy. If it were white instead of black, he could almost look like Santa Claus. Of course, these thoughts didn't enter my mind while I was looking down the barrel of an enemy rifle. They just occurred to me after I awoke. Perhaps if a younger Federal trooper had me in his sights instead of a more mature soldier, the outcome might have been different.

I don't know what the outcome of this skirmish was but I find it hard to believe the Federal troops would have been so charitable toward us, even though we were obviously trying to shoot over their heads. I can recall that the young Federal trooper who tried to hide behind that birch tree was watching me with a big grin on his face. Could it be possible that because there were no officers in my platoon to be of value to take prisoner, and the fact that we looked like a pathetic harmless bunch of men that couldn't even shoot straight, they decided to let us go and move on?

Perhaps the fact that we had a wounded man in the ditch with us also may have been a factor in our fate. I remember staring at that wounded man's face and knowing I couldn't do anything for him because I knew I had no medical skills at all. He didn't seem to be breathing and I know he didn't regain consciousness all the while he lay behind us in that ditch. Since I awoke at that time, I don't know what the final outcome was of our predicament on that hot summer day.

CHAPTER IV

THE FUNERAL

While the dream of the skirmish was still fresh in my mind, at the time I thought of it as nothing more than just a dream. I had not been watching any movies or reading any books to induce such a dream, and yet I found myself right in the middle of a confrontation that could have happened about 140 years ago. Emotions run high during stress and throughout the long and colorful dream I could sense the effects of that strange experience still lingering for a few days.

By the end of the week, which was only four days after the dream of the skirmish in the woods, I found myself once again dreaming of being in the Civil War. It was cool and damp, unlike the irritating heat and humidity of mid-summer of my last dream. Also absent was the running and shooting in a tangled forest of bushes and trees. This time I was with a whole company of Confederate soldiers milling about in a large field. The nearest trees seemed to be about a mile away. The sky was gray and dismal and a strange swirling cloud formation caught my eye way off in the distance. It wasn't a funnel cloud, however, it still made me a little uneasy.

Also, unlike my last dream, the whole company including myself was dressed in uniforms. The wool gray uniform with the brass buttons was very comfortable and offered satisfactory protection against the damp chilly air. As I spoke with our company captain, he seemed very nervous. He was a distinguished looking man with short curly black hair and a small mustache. I would estimate his age to be about 30 and his height was probably about 6 feet tall, although I still had to look down at him, since I was once again the same very tall young sergeant from my last dream.

As we talked, I can remember his fumbling with his saber sword belt buckle, as he didn't seem to realize that the right side of his belt had twisted. This company gathering was assembled to conduct a military funeral to say goodbye and pay our respects to an old loyal friend. She was our company mascot, a mule by the name of Annabelle Lee. The captain told me not to mention this funeral to the other men in the other companies. I don't know whether he feared reprimand or laughter from his superiors, as having a formal military funeral complete with dress uniforms for a mascot was against army regulations. Perhaps the captain's uneasiness was due to emotional stress, as the whole company felt very upset over the loss of our mule.

While we stood there talking I could see the other men walking to an area of the field and began to form a line. I excused myself to the captain and started to walk toward the same area. When I arrived a minute later the men had formed a line of about 20 men and were standing shoulder to shoulder. One of the men had taken the initiative to form a new line and I followed behind him. When we were directly across the men at the end of the other line, we stopped and faced them. As the other men followed along behind us, we soon had two lines of about 20 soldiers in each line standing shoulder to shoulder.

My position in line was the second man from the end. As I awaited the sound of the drum and for the caisson carrying the carcass of our mule to pass before us, I became even more aware of my tall stature. The man on my left and on my right came up to just past my elbows. I could see from looking down the row of men that I seemed to be the tallest man in our line, although I didn't dwell on this at the time. It was just an observation recalled upon awakening. I also became aware of the gaunt faces of some of the men facing me from the other line. The bloodshot eyes and drawn expressions were an indication of either their sorrow for the occasion, or the harsh life of war was taking its toll.

Soon I could hear the tapping of the drum as the drummer droned out a slow beat. We immediately focused our eyes straight ahead and snapped to attention. The caisson carrying the carcass of our mascot was apparently to begin its procession to my right, which meant I was almost at the end of the line. It also meant I would be almost the last man to salute our faithful departed friend. Since I was standing at attention and could only look straight ahead, I couldn't watch the slow procession as it moved past the men who saluted as it went by. All I could think of was I hoped I would be able to restrain my tears until the ceremony was over. It would have been embarrassing to let the other men see me cry.

I could feel the emotion starting to overwhelm me, as I fought back the tears to no avail. As the caisson slowly passed in front of me, I offered a snappy salute and stood rigidly at attention. Suddenly, the tears flowed down my face. It was at this point I awoke to find my face and pillow soaked with tears. I sat up on the edge of the bed, and I still couldn't stop crying. I just repeated over and over to myself that it was just a dream, and anyhow, how could we be so emotionally attached to a mule? After about 15 minutes had passed, I regained my composure, but I never forgot that dream. Had I not been such a regimental soldier and allowed my eyes to observe more of my surroundings, I would no doubt had been able to remember more of the men and the activity around me.

I just couldn't believe I had become so emotional over a dream. I don't know how long I lay there crying in my sleep, but my pillowcase was very wet, as well as my face. For some reason, I found it very difficult to stop crying, even though I knew I was awake and sitting on the edge of the bed. I knew I had to get ready for work, and I tried to put the dream out of my mind. Eventually, I regained my composure and prepared to get ready for work.

I had no more emotional outbursts from the unusual lingering effects of the dream, but I couldn't forget it either. This was the second dream of the Civil War in the same week, and in both dreams I looked like the same tall, thin young soldier. What did it all mean? Why were both dreams so vivid and colorful, and especially so unforgettable? The dream content was very unusual to say the least. A whole military company of men paying sad homage to a dead mule is not exactly your usual run of the mill dream. It's also very strange that I knew the name of the mule without hearing anyone mention her name, and I don't recall seeing a nameplate on the caisson. When you think about it, there isn't a more southern name than Annabelle Lee.

Since my attention was directed straight ahead of me throughout most of that funeral procession, I can still recall some of the faces of the men in the other line who were facing us. In spite of their dress uniforms, their bloodshot eyes and haggard faces were enough to scare the enemy without firing a shot.

I somehow felt we were so attached to that mule because she saved our lives more than once. Maybe she was our pack mule, carrying our much needed food and ammo through enemy fire. Maybe we felt such a love and respect for her simply because she was our mascot, and who in this day and age hasn't shed a tear over the death of a pet dog or cat? I don't really know what was the cause of the death of Annabelle Lee. Perhaps she was hit with enemy fire or just simply died of old age. Anyway, we sure gave her a grand farewell.

CHAPTER V

DREAMS OF PAST LIVES

As the years went by the dreams of my life as a Confederate soldier never recurred. In fact, I never really gave much thought to this being anything but a dream. Occasionally, I would ask my friends or relatives if they ever had a dream that they were living in a different time and looked totally different. I always got a negative answer after a long blank stare. These two dreams haunted my thoughts for years, perhaps because of the clarity of detail, and the strange fact that I looked like an entirely different person. Nevertheless, I just assumed it was nothing more than an unusual dream.

It was the spring of 1993 that I was walking through the Quakerbridge Mall. This is my favorite mall since it is located only about 7 miles from my home in Hamilton Square, a suburb of Trenton, N.J. As I was browsing through the mall, I walked upstairs to Waldenbooks book store.

I walked to the "New Age" section to see if any new books on parapsychology would catch my interest. While scanning the usual selection of books on everything from witchcraft to astrology, one book stood by itself in a less congested area of the shelf. It was a small but thick paperback book entitled, *The Psychic Side of Dreams* by Hans Holzer. Considering the book contained many chapters on dream subjects, such as "ESP Dreams" and "How Dreams Can Improve Your Life" I just happened to open the book to the chapter called "Reincarnation Dreams."

As I started to scan the article, I immediately recognized myself as he described how people can experience a memory of their past lives through dreams. He said the dreamer never looks the way he does now because the dream always deals with the past. It is himself and it is to him that all these things are happening. This was exactly the case with me as I began to recall the two vivid dreams of the Civil War some 15 years ago.

I could only remember parts of the dream that I could see through the eyes of the Confederate soldier. It wasn't as though I were off to the side as an observer of all these happenings. I don't really know what my face looked like because I wasn't looking in a mirror. I was obviously very tall because I had to look down to talk to the men, and I know I was thin. As I lay in the ditch shooting toward the Federal troops, I don't know what was going on behind me. Also, I don't recall what all the men in my platoon looked like, only those I spoke to or were next to me. In other words, if my eyes didn't look in that direction, I don't remember what was there.

Until I read this book, I always assumed a person can only experience reincarnation memories through hypnotic regression. Every book or magazine article I ever read of a person recalling a past life had been accomplished through a hypnotic experience. Then again, the person conducting the hypnosis is often an author involved in case studies of reincarnation. In all probability a person experiencing a dream of living in a past life would only consider it a personal dream event and would not think to share the experience by writing about it.

I was so fascinated by Hans Holzer's book that I wrote

to him to tell him how much I enjoyed his book, and also related in detail my two dreams of my experience in the Confederate Army, which I could still recall after all those passing years. I guess just the fact that I could still remember every detail of a dream after 15 years should have given me a clue that these two dreams were not just ordinary dreams. After all, who can actually recall a dream they had 15 years ago and be able to describe what everyone looked like and the clothes they were wearing not to mention the oppressive heat and humidity. I can remember my biology teacher telling the class that no one dreams in color, only black and white. So much for that theory! I also mentioned my lack of interest and knowledge of Civil War history, so he wouldn't assume it may be my obsession with the subject that spurred these dreams.

His response came within the week of my letter to him in May of 1993. It was in the form of an invitation to visit him in New York City for a hypnosis session to see if we could find out more information as to names, places and any information that could be researched and verified. It was his opinion that this was certainly a reincarnation experience. I must admit that even though I sent a long detailed letter to Dr. Holzer, I wasn't optimistic of receiving a reply, especially one so soon. I assumed his busy schedule left little time to answer personal fan letters, but whether I received a reply or not, I had to tell him how much I enjoyed his books and magazine articles over the years. I also couldn't resist telling him of my two dreams of the Civil War, especially since they were a perfect example of what he wrote about in his book.

Although I was very excited to receive his invitation, I was very apprehensive about subjecting myself to hypnosis. It wasn't that I was afraid of possibly being made a fool of while under hypnosis, as I saw many times on some of the old variety shows on TV. I'm sure many of us remember the hypnotist who asks for a volunteer from the audience who soon becomes the victim of indignity due to the suggestions of the hypnotist. I was well aware of Dr. Holzer's long successful experience in hypnosis, as well as his serious dedication to recording for future study, the results of these hypnosis sessions.

I thanked him for his invitation and told him I would let him know. As the weeks went by I thought more and more about meeting Hans Holzer. I've been such a fan of his books and magazine articles for so many years, and yet I was concerned about not only the after effects of hypnosis, but also about trying to find his apartment building in all the chaotic maze of New York City. I have never really been much of a traveler, and the very thought of being lost in a gridlock of traffic in the Big Apple started to make me think twice about this whole idea. As the weeks went by, I managed to come by several books that dealt with the subject of hypnosis. The more I read of people's experience with hypnosis, the more I was left with the impression that, when performed by an experienced and competent hypnotist, the procedure seemed relatively safe.

Now that my apprehension of being hypnotized had abated, my driving to New York City was still a big concern for me. I didn't know of anyone who knew his way around the Big Apple, so I couldn't seek help of my friends or family. One day while browsing through the telephone book, I saw the answer to my problem, as several limo services were advertised. I have never rented a limo before, and I knew the cost of traveling even a short distance in one of these could be exorbitant. Nevertheless, I thought it wouldn't cost anything to call and get some information on their rates. I told them I was not interested in making a grand entrance to impress anyone, I just wanted basic transportation to New York

City with a driver who knew his way around. After getting what seemed like a surprisingly fair rate estimate on the phone, I told them I would call back to make definite arrangements.

Now that I had allayed my fear of hypnosis and seemed to have transportation arrangements at my disposal, I telephoned Hans Holzer to make an appointment to meet him. Now it was the 23rd of October and almost five months had passed since we last corresponded, and much to my surprise he remembered me. As soon as I identified myself to him, his response was, "Oh, you're the Confederate sergeant." I couldn't believe that after five months he actually remembered me from my letter. I know he is a busy man but I was fortunate that he was able to see me in just a few days. I thought it would take at least a few weeks.

The next day I called the limo service to have someone pick me up at my house on the designated day. My appointment was for 3:30 PM on that warm and sunny October 25th, and the limo driver picked me up at 1:30 PM to allow enough time to travel the 75 miles or so to the traffic infested city. When the driver arrived, I realized why the rates were so reasonable. As I left my house to approach the car, the driver was busy picking up the license plate that had fallen off and reattached it.

As he scurried to the passenger door and opened it for me, it creaked and groaned. The limo turned out to be an old Crown Victoria whose many miles were beginning to show. The driver was a thin elderly gentleman dressed in typical dark chauffeur attire. As he held the rear door open for me, I asked him if it would be permissible to sit in the front seat. It was going to be a long ride and I thought we could converse a lot easier if we were sitting next to each other. The front passenger seat seemed to be loaded with paraphernalia, including the credit card transactor. Apparently, no one has ever requested to sit up front before. When we finally gathered up everything from the front seat and put it in the back seat, he held the front door open for me. As I sat down I noticed he didn't remove quite everything. Between us sat a bag of jelly beans, which he indulged occasionally on the long drive up and back.

He turned out to be not only an excellent driver but a good driving companion as well. Since he drove this route many times before, he was familiar with the traffic patterns and the pit stops. The weather was unseasonably warm for the end of October, and we both agreed we would feel more comfortable with the air conditioner on. Before I knew it we were in New York City with its busy streets of trucks and cabs. I felt very relieved that I wasn't driving my car while trying to find an address in this busy city.

We made it to Hans Holzer's apartment building with 15 minutes to spare. I assumed we were going to have to look for a parking lot, but as luck would have it we found a curb side parking space right across the street. As he held the door open for me, I grabbed my small valice containing my little tape recorder and Dr. Holzer's latest book, in anticipation of having him autograph it for me. As I headed across the street, the driver told me he would take a brief nap while I was gone. It was comforting to know that I wouldn't have to drive home during the hectic rush hour. I was not completely at ease to begin with, and I didn't know how I would feel after the hypnosis.

CHAPTER VI

THE HYPNOSIS

When I arrived at Dr. Holzer's apartment in Manhattan he greeted me at the door. I found him to be a very likeable gentleman as well as very intelligent, as his many scholarly degrees that adorned his wall would attest. He made it clear to me in a previous letter that there would be no guarantees that I could be regressed sufficiently to recall my identity and the location of the skirmish I was in during the Civil War dream. Some people are more susceptible to hypnotic suggestions than others, but I knew Dr. Holzer has had many years experience with hypnosis. If the session didn't bring the desired results, I knew I must be one of those subjects who just can't experience a deep hypnosis.

He invited me to sit on a cot across from his desk while he sat in a chair. I was beginning to feel more at ease, as we talked of some of his past books and magazine articles, subjects that were of particular interest to me. However, it was time to get down to business and he asked me if I had brought a tape recorder. I said I had and I even made sure the batteries were new. I reached in my valice and remembered there was one more item I wanted to take care of, his autograph of his latest book at that time, *America's Restless Ghosts*. This book contained some amazing photographs of ghosts and other extraordinary manifestations, such as clouds and swirls of ectoplastic energy that were not visible when the photo was taken. He graciously signed my book and I put it back in my valice and set my tape recorder on the floor next to the cot.

As I lay on the cot with the tape recorder within easy reach, he began to talk to relax me. I tried to block out the noises of the traffic below and concentrate only on his voice. His suggestions that I was becoming more and more relaxed, and that I was floating over a field on a warm sunny day did indeed put me at ease. After a few moments of these mind relaxing exercises he began to ask me questions relating to my life in the Confederate Army. He was probing me to find out my name and location while under the influence of hypnosis, although I realized I was not fully regressed. I lay there with my eyes closed and was in complete compliance with Dr. Holzer's suggestions, although if someone in the apartment building yelled "FIRE" I would have been up and out the door in no time.

As he continued to ask me questions of my life in the Confederate Army, I suddenly felt like I was back in the woods during the skirmish with the Federal troops. It was as if I were back in my dream again, but yet I had enough control of my own mind to know where I was and that this mental vision was all part of the hypnosis.

I immediately told Dr. Holzer of the vision before me, and he began to direct his questions pertaining to my situation in the woods. I began to answer his questions by replying whatever name came to my mind. My response to his question of my identity was Sgt. Albert Richardson. When he asked me what regiment I was attached to I told him I was with a Virginia regiment. He also asked me the location of the skirmish in the woods that was going on in my mind at that time, and I told him I was in Maryland. When he asked me my place of birth,

I answered Roanoke, Virginia. I knew I wasn't fully regressed but I answered his questions with the information that was going on in my mind at that time.

Shortly before he decided to bring me back to a normal and fully awake state of mind, he kept probing me as to what my mission was, and asked me if there was something that I was supposed to do but failed to do. I suddenly began to feel very guilty because I knew I was the sergeant in charge of this platoon of men, and I believe I made some very bad decisions to put the lives of these men in such a bad situation.

As Dr. Holzer suggested I return to the present, I became fully awake but was a little misty eyed from the emotional impact of that experience, and I started to feel that I may have caused the loss of our whole platoon due to my irrational decisions. When Dr. Holzer detected that I was a little upset over this experience, he told me to lie down again and suggested I would feel very good and would not be upset over this experience. It seemed to work, because as I arose from the cot to a sitting position, I felt very relaxed but extremely thirsty. It took two large glasses of that delicious New York City water to quench my thirst. Could it have been because of my re-living that war experience on that extremely hot and humid day?

When the hypnosis session came to a close, Dr. Holzer told me I would gradually remember who I was and that memories would come back to me in the form of more dreams and quick mental flashbacks. He advised me to keep a pen and pad handy next to my bed to record these dream events as they happened so I wouldn't forget them. I started to smile in disbelief but he assured me he was quite serious about keeping the pad and pen handy. Since I felt I didn't make a very good subject of hypnosis, I had my doubts that I would ever have need for the pad and pen for that purpose, but I told Dr. Holzer I would follow his advice.

During the hypnosis, the vision of the skirmish first appeared to me as if I were sitting in the front row of a movie theater watching the event unfold before me in all of its brilliant colors, but it was as if I were quickly absorbed into the action. I especially remember reliving that part of the dream where the Federal trooper stood up from behind that bush and aimed his rifle at my face. It seems the trauma we face in our lives imprints a memory like a scar from a branding iron, and becomes a memory in our next life. Dr. Holzer also suggested that I do some research to see if I could find any information to verify the existence of an Albert Richardson, who may have lived in Roanoke, Virginia. Since I was not in a complete regressed state of hypnosis, I had my doubts about the names and places that were passing through my mind as being historical fact, but then again I didn't really know.

As I stood up from the cot and gathered my tape recorder and valice, I felt fine but still a little bewildered. Dr. Holzer once again reminded me of the importance of keeping a pad and pen handy as he led me out the door to the elevator. As we shook hands I stepped aboard the elevator and was soon back out on the street.

The limo driver saw me leaving the building and was waiting for me with the door open. As I entered the limo the driver commented that we'd no doubt encounter a gridlock of traffic on our way home, as it was close to 5:00 PM. As he drove he pointed out some of the landmarks on the New York City skyline. He said it was very unusual to actually be able to see the skyline so clearly, as it is usually obscured by fog and haze. As we approached the Holland Tunnel, we prepared for the usual gridlock at rush hour, but to our amazement the traffic was extremely light. Even the weather still continued to cooperate, as we once again had to use the air conditioner on the way home.

On the way home I began to think about the hour and a half I spent with Dr. Holzer. I couldn't help but feel a little disappointed at myself for not being able to relive that life in the Confederate Army for awhile. I would have been able to offer more factual information that could be more easily verified if I were able to reach such a state of hypnotic regression. Of course, I was very pleased to be able to meet the famous author whose work I have always found interesting and fascinating. Even if the whole experiment turned out to be a disappointment, it was well worth the trip.

As I reflected on the answers I gave him while under hypnosis, I was surprised at myself when I told him the skirmish was in Maryland. My knowledge of the Civil War was indeed limited, but I didn't remember reading or hearing of any Civil War battles fought in Maryland, and I began to feel very foolish. If I were answering his questions just for the sake of having an answer, why in the world did I pick Maryland? I felt much better when my research later uncovered a fact I never knew. When General Lee's Army of Northern Virginia was retreating from the battle of Gettysburg, at least eight battles or skirmishes took place in Maryland. Also, at the time, I had never heard of the battle at Antietam, which of course was not only fought in Maryland, but had one of the highest list of casualties in any battle of the Civil War.

The rest of the trip home seemed to take only half the time as the trip to New York City, and when he finally dropped me off in front of my house, I thought about how well everything went this day. It all seemed like a good omen that I was meant to make this trip. When I arrived home I paid the limo driver with a credit card and jumped into my car and headed for a fast food restaurant, as I was famished. When I returned home, I was anxious to play back the tape. As I did, I found little interest in my responses to Dr. Holzer's questions. The main reason to have a tape recorder at these hypnosis sessions is to record a possible total regression, where the subject becomes a different person, often with a different voice. At a successful regression a lot of past information is often recorded, which the subject can later use to trace and verify his past life. My responses were brief and barely audible.

I was very tired when I went to bed that night, as if I had an exhausting day. I didn't know what to expect in the way of dreams, however the night produced only a sound sleep. It seems that Dr. Holzer's hypnotic suggestion that I would have dreams and flashbacks of the Civil War was more successful than the actual attempt at deep hypnotic regression. The dreams and flashbacks started the next day.

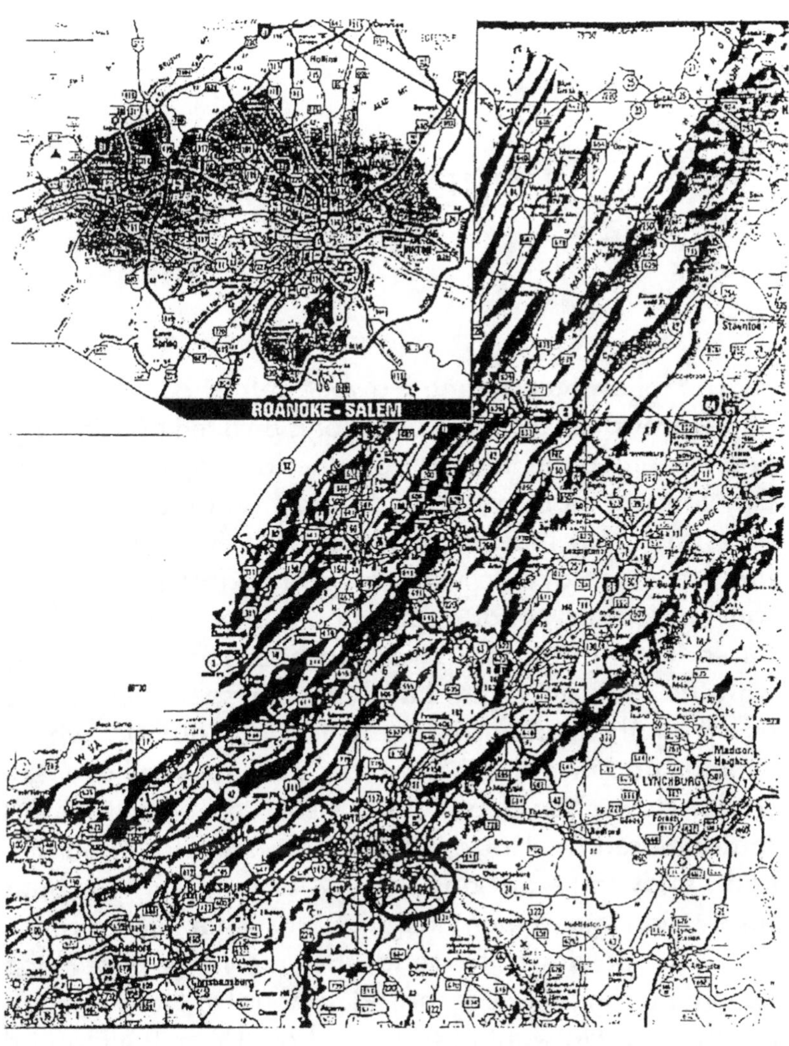

The circled area and the inset is the city of Roanoke, the city that immediately came to my mind while under hypnosis when I was asked by Dr. Holzer where I was born.

CHAPTER VII

THE BRIDGE

The following morning I awoke refreshed. The events of the previous day were full of long awaited anticipation, and it seemed the tension from the journey to New York City left me more exhausted than I realized. As I went about my daily morning routine, I felt fine. I thought of the previous day's activities over breakfast and my visit with Dr. Holzer. My disappointment in not being able to attain a total state of regression had begun to subside with the realization that I had actually spent almost two hours in the company of my favorite author, whose writings and investigative research is known all over the world. How often does one get such an opportunity? I remembered Dr. Holzer's advice on keeping a pen and pad handy to record any dreams of the Civil War but I surely didn't need them last night, as I slept like a rock.

As I sat down to read the morning paper the telephone rang. I was surprised to hear Dr. Holzer's voice on the line. He wanted to know how I was feeling and also if I had any dreams last night. I told him I was fine but I slept so soundly I don't believe I had any dreams. He reminded me once more to take notes on any dreams that may occur. I assured him I would do just that. I looked at the time and saw that it was 10AM.

Late that afternoon I decided to read some of the

book Dr. Holzer had given me. It was one of his earlier books entitled, *Born Again*. I read in an article in a magazine that it was recommended reading for anyone who is interested in reincarnation, and I found it to be unavailable in book stores. I mentioned to him at our meeting that I had tried in vain to find his book anywhere because it is out of print. A quick search of his vast collection of books produced the book, which he graciously gave to me as a gift. It is an interesting account of some of his investigations of people who claim they have had some kind of experience with a past life, either nagging memories or dreams. The detailed events that are revealed of a past life by many of Dr. Holzer's participants in his hypnotic regression sessions are fascinating. I was thoroughly engrossed in reading this fascinating book but suddenly found I couldn't keep my eyes open.

In the next instant I found myself standing on the bank of a canal looking up at a black wooden bridge. It was night time and the full moon was peeking in and out of the clouds. I seemed to be studying its structure, and I could see that it appeared to have just been painted with a high gloss black paint. As the full moon peeked from the passing clouds, it reflected on the glossy wet look of the black paint.

The bridge was about 20 feet high with a cross beam structured railing extending about 8 feet above the path of the bridge. It was wide enough to accommodate the passing of two horse and carriages, and it tapered down to meet the ground. It was not a railroad bridge, but appeared to be strong enough to allow troops and supplies to cross.

I was accompanied by about 6 men who were very busy carrying wooden kegs of gunpowder. I walked away from the base of the bridge toward the men to help with the kegs of gunpowder. We had to work in high weeds and one of the men flattened out some of the weeds and sat down with his legs outstretched and apart with a keg of gunpowder between them. He seemed to be doing something with the top of each keg as we brought the kegs to him. As the full moon shown down upon one of the men carrying a keg of gunpowder, I could see that he was wearing gray pants, a shirt with long baggy sleeves and a yellow or tan round hat with a very large wide brim.

I didn't feel in charge or responsible for these men as I did in the other two dreams. I just felt as a part of the team. We were working quickly and quietly, not saying a word to each other, and working only by the light of the full moon.

When I awoke from my brief nap and tried to analyze our purpose in the dream, I can only assume we were going to attempt to destroy the bridge. I couldn't see what the man was doing with the tops of those kegs of gunpowder, but he may have been placing a fuse or somehow preparing to make them explosive. My reading of the Civil War reference books made me aware that it was a common practice to blow up bridges that the enemy would have access. The fact that we didn't use lanterns and we didn't speak a word to each other leads me to believe we may have been carrying out this mission right under the noses of the Federal troops.

While the details of my brief dream were still fresh in my mind, I wrote them down on a pad. It was such a strange feeling to be sitting in my living room reading a book, and the next minute finding myself looking up at a wooden bridge in the moonlight. The sight of that bridge and the full moon gave me an eerie feeling. We didn't have the full benefit of the light of the moon, as it was intermittently covered by the passing clouds. As I stood in those high weeds and looked out over the water, I couldn't tell whether we were standing next to a river or a canal, as it was too dark to see across to the other side.

Since I was the only one standing at the base of the bridge and seemed to be studying its architectural structure, maybe I was the one to determine where the kegs of gunpowder should be placed. As I trudged through the high weeds, I found it to be an effort even for my long legs, as I was once again the very tall thin soldier.

As I lifted a keg of gunpowder up from the weeds to my stomach, I realized how heavy those kegs were. We were fortunate that the weather was favorable, as it felt like a comfortable evening in early summer. Had it been raining we would probably have been bogged down in the mud. The dream was too brief to determine the success of our mission that night, but everything seemed to be going along smoothly.

CHAPTER VIII

THE BATTLEFIELD

After I sent Dr. Holzer a note explaining the details of my dream of the bridge, I didn't really know what to expect next. Perhaps the after effects of the hypnosis was still with me, or perhaps just hearing Dr. Holzer's voice again on the phone may have induced the suggestion of another Civil War dream.

Although my meeting with Dr. Holzer was an exciting experience for me, I must admit I was a little disappointed in myself for not satisfying my original desire to be completely regressed to a point where I wouldn't even be aware of being in Dr. Holzer's apartment building in New York City here in the twentieth century. I was hoping for the ultimate experience of re-living my past life in the Confederate Army, just as Mrs. Virginia Tighe was re-living her past life in eighteenth century Ireland. I wanted to be able to give Dr. Holzer more conclusive information about my past identity, rather than names that just passed through my mind while I was still clinging to the present.

The dreams I had experienced at this point were far too unusual to be just dreams, I was convinced of this. All three dreams so far were vivid and colorful, and who could dismiss the fact that I looked like the same tall, lanky soldier in each dream, a far cry from my present physical being. Since my first two dreams occurred so many years ago, and it took a session of hypnosis to induce another dream after all these years, I thought that possibly this would be the end of my dreams about the Civil War. I was soon to learn that this was just the beginning.

About two weeks had passed since the dream about the bridge, and I began to slowly put the dreams of the Civil War out of my mind. After all, wouldn't I have had several more dreams by this time? Perhaps I was right in assuming it was probably the sound of Dr. Holzer's voice on the telephone that induced my last dream experience of the bridge. That dream had haunted my thoughts for the past few weeks, and I knew it would probably haunt me for many years to come.

One cold November morning after having breakfast, I sat on my living room sofa and started to read the morning newspaper. While reading of the recent events of the day, my eyes suddenly closed, and I found myself running across a spacious field with a large group of Confederate soldiers. We were charging across a dry dusty field that appeared to be strewn with hay or straw. The sun was so hot and the sky was a clear light blue. We were definitely the aggressors in this battle, as we charged across the field and up a slight hill, clutching our rifles and yelling at the top of our lungs. I felt so confident we were going to win this battle, I actually felt euphoric.

Although I was spared the memory of bayoneting anyone, we were engaged in hand to hand combat. I was in the front line and the Confederate soldier on my left was our flag bearer. He seemed to stay by my side all throughout the fighting. He was close enough to me that the flag he was carrying was partially obscuring my view.

The flag was large and appeared to have a yellow background with a red emblem or design. Since there was no wind, the flag was hanging down and partially draped around the flag pole. At this point I awoke.

As I sat there on the sofa with the newspaper on my lap, I realized it had just happened again. I instinctively reached for a pad and pen and began to jot down notes while the startling details of the dream were still fresh in my mind. One part of that dream that puzzled me was the color of our flag. I had always seen pictures of the Confederate flag as being red with a wide band of blue cross bars of white stars. The flag was clearly yellow and red in my dream, even though I couldn't distinguish the design or pattern of the red emblem. What kind of flag were we carrying anyway?

A trip to the mall book store the next day turned out to be a rewarding experience. I headed straight for the "History"aisle and hoped I would find some answers to the puzzling question concerning the colors of our flag. The selection available consisted of many books on the Civil War, but I would need one with colorful illustrations, as black and white photos would do me no good. I didn't know if I would find what I was looking for, as most of the artists' paintings I have seen portraying battle scenes usually depicted the traditional Confederate flag.

Suddenly, I spotted a large book entitled, *Arms & Equipment of the Confederacy*, by Time-Life Books. As I slid it out of the shelf I could see the cover was an arrangement of color photos of uniforms, weapons and a flag. I knew this must be the book I am looking for. As I cradled the large book in my arms and began flipping through the pages of colorful photos, I came to a chapter devoted only to flags. I couldn't believe my luck! I never knew there was such a variety of Confederate flags. I thought the South fought under only one flag. Again, my ignorance of Civil War history was being made evident.

I finally turned to a page that contained a color photo of a tattered yellow flag with a red square in the upper left corner. Within the square was the traditional blue bars and white stars. It was the second national regimental battle flag, of which many were sent to regiments that joined the Army of Northern Virginia. I believe this may have been the flag in my dream. I have to bear in mind that the color photos of the flags were those of flags already many years old and probably some discoloration would take place after all those years. The gold color of some of the flags may have faded to a light yellow, or a red color may have faded to a very light pink. The flag that was draped near my face in my dream was a new flag with a lemon yellow background and what we would call today a fire engine red. Even though I couldn't see the red symbol or design on the flag due to the absence of wind, and because I was so focused on the Federal troops in front of me, I came to the conclusion that the flag was probably from the Army of Northern Virginia, due to the illustration in that reference book

At this point, unfortunately I don't know where this battle took place. I only saw the dust from the dry field, our flag and the wave of blue uniformed troops trying to repel our attack. My attention during this entire battle was focused straight ahead toward the enemy. That is why the flag obscuring my vision caused me some concern. I didn't want to be stabbed with a bayonet because I was not able to see it coming. I wanted to be able to see clearly to defend myself.

Even though this dream was very brief, it also was so vivid and detailed. The field we were fighting on was strewn with what appeared to be dry, light brown leaves, but they were probably dried up corn husks, and not hay or straw as I first thought. As we were running up that hill, I'll never forget the surprised look on the faces of those young Federal troops as we met them face to face on the ridge of that hill. They seemed to be just rising from a sitting position and looked at us with their eyes wide open and their jaws dropped.

Since my concentration was straight ahead of me, I don't recall if we were wearing uniforms, but the Federal troops seemed dressed more for a parade than for battle, as they didn't have a button or a buckle out of place. Our flag bearer was making me nervous by staying so close to me. Even though there didn't seem to be a breeze that day, he always managed to lower that huge yellow flag in my face. We were so clustered together fighting shoulder to shoulder that I guess it couldn't be helped, but I didn't want to take my eyes off those Federal troops for a second.

Even though this dream was brief and unexpected, it was so vivid and colorful. I don't usually fall asleep and dream in the middle of the day, and yet this was the second time this has happened to me. Of course, the content of both of these dreams left me with no doubt that the effects of the hypnosis was still with me. I don't know what the catalyst for that last dream was, as I assumed my conversation on the phone with Dr. Holzer may have induced the dream of the bridge. I have sat in my yard or my living room many times while reading a book or newspaper and although I find this usually is relaxing, I have never been suddenly projected to the past. In both instances the dreams came to me so suddenly I barely had time to close my eyes.

I realized that Dr. Holzer was correct when he advised me to keep a pen and pad handy, as these dreams and flashbacks of the Civil War would occur. It had been two weeks since the last dream of the Civil War, and I didn't know if or when there would be another. Just as I did after the vivid dream of the bridge, I wrote to Dr. Holzer and explained in detail my latest escapade in the Civil War. Of course, I don't know what the outcome of this battle was, but considering the large amount of troops involved in this battle, perhaps we left our mark in history on that day.

CHAPTER IX

THE WHEATFIELD

At this time I noticed a pattern of time between dreams, for it was early December and it was just about two weeks again before the next dream of the Civil War occurred. Compared to the action and emotional tension of some of my past life dreams, this one was tranquil. It was very brief and vivid but seemed rather pointless to me at the time. I soon came to the conclusion that this dream was introduced to me primarily as a learning experience.

The dream began as I found myself walking through a dense woods. It may have been in the autumn season, as the trees were sparse of leaves. It was daytime but the sky was overcast and the air had a slight chill. I was alone and as I made my way through the underbrush I could see a clearing ahead. When I was within about 100 feet of the clearing I could see that it was a wheatfield. Just ahead of me stood a thick gnarled tree that grew at the edge of the woods. Closer observation of the wheatfield revealed just how large it was, as it bordered the woods on my right in a horseshoe shape, where the trees ended abruptly. The wheatfield that lay beyond that patch of trees seemed endless.

At this time I noticed a Confederate soldier off to my left. He was standing knee high in the wheat about 40 feet from the edge of the woods. He didn't seem to be aware of my presence, as I had not emerged from the woods, and his attention was away from me toward the open field for the most part. As I headed in his direction I could see he had a small mustache and appeared to be in his early 30's. He was carrying his rifle in his left hand and appeared to be lost in thought as he gazed across the wheatfield. Perhaps he was thinking of his family back home. He apparently had not been in recent battle, as he was dressed in full clean uniform and appeared to be physically fit. I didn't find this to be unusual at the time of the dream, but he was wearing a tan uniform that appeared to have some kind of red ornamentation on his belt and on his tan hat. Strangely enough, this dream occurred again the following night.

I thought it was strange that this dream would repeat itself the following night. It was then that I realized that perhaps this dream was shown to me twice for a reason. It certainly wasn't a nightmare that was so upsetting as to cause lingering emotional effects, and perhaps cause a repeat of that dream. I began to mentally retrace my steps through the dream and try to analyze its significance. What was its purpose? I just couldn't help but wonder about that soldier's uniform. Why was he wearing a tan uniform instead of gray, and what was that red ornamentation around his belt and on top of his hat? I thought perhaps he was in a special brigade. His jacket was short and tight fitting, and the two rows of small brass buttons seemed to cause a row of creases across his chest. Even his posture suggested time at West Point. These questions bothered me and I knew I had to try to find the answers.

About a week later I was back at the mall book store. As I scanned the selection of books on the Civil War, I noticed a large variety of books called, *Men-at-Arms Series*. I was fortunate to find that one of the books contained color illustrations of Confederate uniforms. I was so surprised to see such a variety of uniforms. I finally came to the page that held the answer to my question. It was a colorful illustration of a 2nd Lieutenant in the Artillery Division wearing a red sash under his ammo belt. Also, the top of his hat was red and gold. This book by Katcher and Volstad became the answer to my perplexing dream puzzle.

Although the uniform was gray in this particular illustration, I found that tan uniforms were also worn. My research concerning the wearing of tan uniforms indicates that before 1864, a light brown was even more common than gray for Confederate uniforms. The wool for the uniforms was dyed with a mixture of the oily nut of the butternut tree and a bluish green crystal known as copperas. The Confederates eventually had access to a regular supply of gray dye and by 1864 began producing only gray uniforms. Another explanation for their having so many tan uniforms was that even vegetable-dyed gray oxidizes over time and becomes tan. Perhaps the fact that this soldier was an officer explains his maturity as well as his clean dignified appearance.

A few nights after this dream, I had a brief but vivid image of a young boy standing next to a cannon. He was carrying a long pole with a swathe of cloth on the end of it over his right shoulder. He appeared to be tired as his glazed eyes seemed to lack any emotion. He didn't seem to be afraid in spite of the fact that the field was so full of white smoke. I could only see him and the cannon. I couldn't even determine if it was night or day. His unbuttoned coat revealed a vest under his gray uniform, and he appeared to be wearing strips of white cloth around his legs below the knees. In spite of the harsh army life, he appeared to be well fed, as his round face and protruding stomach would indicate.

This image appeared to me while falling asleep at

bedtime. It wasn't quite a dream but more of a flashback. The image came on too quickly for me to actually call this a dream, but as quickly as it flashed across my sleepy conscious it disappeared. If this was part of a memory of a scene on a battlefield, it must have not only been a furious battle due to all the white smoke, it must have been a desperate battle. This boy looked no older than a drummer boy, perhaps about 12 years old. Perhaps he abandoned his drum to assist in the firing of the cannon. Since I seemed to be observing him from a distance of only about 10 feet and he paid no attention to me, I can assume he had his mind only on the task at hand.

This brief flashback of that boy trying to help man that cannon during that terrible battle still haunts me. I realize it was probably common practice to recruit a young boy to play the drums for the soldiers to keep up the morale during battle and during the long marches to their destinations. It just makes me wonder how the parents of a boy so young would let him go off to war carrying nothing but a drum. I can't understand why the army of either side would consent to subjecting him to the obvious dangers that were encountered all through the war. When the artillery shells start flying there is no guarantee for anyone's safety. Perhaps these drummer boys were orphans and the army was their only family.

Several months after this dream image occurred, I found a photo of a drummer boy in a Civil War reference book at a book store. I noticed he was wearing white leggings and spats, much like the infantry soldiers of World War 1. The white strips of cloth I saw on the drummer boy's legs in my dream vision were probably the same type of leggings I saw in that book.

Even though the North won the war, it's interesting to note that the last surviving veteran of the Civil War was from the South. As I recall, he was a drummer boy who died in 1959 at the age of 109. 1 don't recall if our local newspaper carried this story or if I read it in one of the popular magazines at that time. I do recall that of the last two surviving veterans, one was a lieutenant in the Union Cavalry. The article about these last two survivors showed a photo of the Union lieutenant in uniform at the age of 123, lying on a bed and petting a fawn. I believe his death came not long before the death of the drummer boy from the South.

Although the last recognized veteran of the Civil War had passed on in 1959, 1 assume there may have been many people living at that time who were 100 years of age or older who were children at the time of the Civil War, but may have still carried those childhood memories with them throughout their lives. Perhaps some of them lived in the South during their childhood and may have remembered getting caught in a crossfire of a skirmish, or remember their homes being burned by the Federal troops. Even though the politics of war meant nothing to them, memories of violence are not easily forgotten.

On one of my favorite TV shows of the 1950's, "I've Got A Secret" with the host Garry Moore, a very memorable guest appeared. As this old man was helped to the seat next to Garry Moore to be questioned by a panel of TV celebrities who tried to guess his secret, the secret was revealed only to the audience and the home viewers. You can imagine the gasp and applause when his secret revealed, "I saw Booth shoot Lincoln." I don't recall if the panel guessed his secret, but at the end of the game it was revealed that this old man was only 5 years old at the time of that fateful night. His parents had taken him to Ford Theater that night and, after hearing the fatal shot, he saw Booth jump from the balcony onto the stage. Not being aware of what had just taken place, he said he remembered feeling sorry for the man because he hurt his leg when he jumped and ran limping off stage. As I recall, this guest was 95 years old at the time of his appearance on this show, so it must have aired in 1955.

I'm sure by this time all of those people who were born in this country before the Civil War have passed on, perhaps only to be reborn another day with their memories still intact.

CHAPTER X

THE CAMPSITE

It was January of 1994 and several weeks had gone by until I found myself again back in the Civil War. My platoon and I had just arrived at the edge of a small town. It was nighttime and a light steady rain was falling. we had decided to rest for the night, and the men split up in search of a tree to sit under to get some shelter from the rain. Three of the men immediately headed for a big chestnut tree about 50 feet away. One of the men lit a lantern he had with him, illuminating themselves and the nearby buildings of the town. Three other groups had walked off into the darkness, and as a glow of light appeared about 100 feet away, I could see three men had taken shelter under a tree. Suddenly another glow of light appeared a short distance from that group. Apparently everyone had picked a place to rest for the night. I don't know if the men camped in the distance also had lanterns or they managed to start a fire in spite of the rain. As for myself, I was too nervous to sit and relax, and I decided to keep watch.

The three men under the chestnut tree looked exhausted, with the exception of one husky young man who appeared to be about 18 years of age. I could see by the light of the lantern he had short dark curly hair. Although it was raining now, we must have walked through days of scorching sun, as his face appeared to be sunburned. He had a look of youthful confidence, as his dark eyes sparkled in the lantern light. He was wearing white or gray baggy pants, a long sleeve shirt and a vest. His back was resting against the tree, and he sat there with his legs outstretched and his ankles crossed. He appeared to be in good spirits, as he talked on and on to the other two men, who looked as if they could hardly stay awake. He may have been a new recruit who had not as yet experienced the shock of bloody battle.

My feelings for the men went beyond a sergeant giving orders that must be obeyed. I felt a deep personal responsibility for each man, and I was only trying to make the best decisions to do our job as soldiers, as well as trying to keep my men and myself alive. Most of the time we were so overwhelmed and outnumbered by the Federal troops that we found ourselves usually on the defensive, running and hiding whenever it was wise to do so in order to stay alive.

While the men relaxed by their lanterns, I was pacing nervously while keeping a watchful eye on the dirt road that led through the small town. I was wearing a poncho type garment with a pleated cape extending across my shoulders and back, that covered my arms about down to the elbows. I was wearing my gray hat and was carrying my rifle. I could see a large concrete building about 50 feet from the chestnut tree. It was about 25 feet high at the peak of the roof which seemed to have a faded red trim. The roof was short in the back of the building and long in the front. Since I was standing facing the side of the building and it was nighttime, I couldn't see any signs, but it could have been a warehouse or a blacksmith shop.

Even though it was nighttime and raining, I could still see part way down the street, and there appeared to be no lights in any of the buildings as far as I could see.

"I do know that if we were to have a confrontation, the Federal Troops would be coming down that dirt road from the other side of town."

Most of the buildings appeared to be stores or businesses on the left side of the street. On the right side of the narrow dirt road appeared a row of wooden houses or eating places, but I saw no signs above the porch entrances to indicate they were used for any kind of business. However, that side of the street was darker for some reason, so perhaps I couldn't see any signs if they were posted. All they appeared to be to me were a row of old shanty houses.

On the left side of the street I could see a long wooden sign on top of the third building down from the warehouse, but at this angle and the lack of light I couldn't read it. I could make out some of the letters on that sign, enough to know it was painted with a light green paint. Perhaps the sign and the trim on the roof of the warehouse were not painted with a light shade of color, but just faded from the weather.

I could see the wooden sidewalks and the hitching posts along the front of these buildings. The hitching post in front of the warehouse looked new, as the edge of the round post appeared to be freshly cut. It also appeared to be white, as if it hadn't been exposed to weather extremes. My interest was not in the town, but the pursuing Federal troops. I seemed to be expecting the Union Cavalry to come riding down that dirt road from the other side of town. I strained my eyes in the darkness looking for any signs of motion or any unusual noises that would seem suspicious in a small quiet town in the middle of the night. I was also listening for the sound of horses' hooves. Although I couldn't see what type of buildings were at the other end of that dirt road, I'm sure the town was very small. I wouldn't have had much warning if the Union Cavalry came down on us at a full gallop. By the time I could even hear them in the darkness it would have been too late.

My platoon needed their rest and at that moment they

were too scattered about to put up much of a defense. My vigilance of the road was punctuated with an occasional walk back to the men under the chestnut tree. Two of the men were sitting on either a log or the root of the tree with their heads bowed and their rifles propped up against their knees. Meanwhile, the young man was still sitting under the tree with his back resting against the trunk. His hands were clasped behind his head and his legs still outstretched with his ankles crossed. I couldn't get over how refreshed he looked as he never stopped talking. He seemed to be unaware of the danger and appeared to be thoroughly enjoying himself. I didn't engage in any conversation with the men and I was too uptight to even concentrate on what the young man was talking so much about. I didn't stay with these men for more than a few minutes at a time, as I wanted to maintain my vigilance of the road. My dream ended as I paced back and forth watching that dark road and waiting.

This seems to be the first dream of the Civil War that I wasn't in a field or the woods. The buildings in that small town were remembered in such detail because my attention was focused on the road that ran through it. As the dream haunted me for days after, I began to wonder why the platoon was so scattered about when we camped that night. I also wondered that perhaps there was a military or safety reason why there were only 3 men to a lantern. It dawned on me later that the reason for our being scattered about that way was because of the rain, and they were seeking out a tree for shelter. I don't remember any of the men carrying tents, but if they had them we didn't use them that night. Considering my uneasiness, we may have been reluctant to get too relaxed, as we may have had to fight or run at any time.

Since the town was so dark and quiet, perhaps there was no saloon in that town, or we may have just arrived at that particular place in the very early hours of the morning before sunrise. I don't know whether I felt we were being pursued by the Federal troops due to a retreat from a recent battle, or whether we were in enemy territory, and I felt a sense of danger simply because of our being there. I do know that if we were to have a confrontation, the Federal troops would be coming down that dirt road from the other side of town.

It is so unusual to experience a dream so vivid that I can remember the constant light rainfall, and even the rough concrete exterior of that building I assumed to be a warehouse. As I paced nervously back and forth to the men under the chestnut tree and back to the street entrance, I held on to my rifle as if it were glued to my hand. I don't know how far we walked that day but I was too uptight to sit and rest. The other men didn't seem to be concerned about a confrontation with the Federal troops, as they just wanted to sit and relax. Maybe I was worrying needlessly, but I felt I owed it to the platoon to be cautious and ready.

Perhaps the old wooden houses across the street were the living quarters of the merchants who owned the businesses on the left side of the street. I couldn't see a flicker of a candle or a trace of light from a kerosene lamp in any of those buildings, but I think the low rain clouds may have made those buildings more visible than if it were a dark clear moonless night. If you ever noticed, it doesn't seem as dark at night when it is cloudy, and perhaps our lantern threw off enough light to enable me to see as much as I did. I don't know how long we stayed at the edge of town. Perhaps we only stopped to rest for a brief time and moved on.

I have no idea where we were camped that night, but every time I browse through a book of old Civil War photographs by Mathew Bradey or other photographers of that time period, I'm always looking for that small town from my dream. I also find myself trying to find a bridge in those old photographs similar to the one in my other dream. I thought both would give me a clue as to what state I was in at the time of my dream. In all probability, there are no existing photographs of that small town, but I keep looking anyway. If that little town did exist as I believe it did, it's probably a shopping mall or an apartment complex today. Of course, there is always the possibility that little town may have developed into a thriving major city. I'm still going to keep my eyes open. Maybe some historian has some photos or old records of their city that was once the little town where a straggling platoon of Confederates once camped for the night.

CHAPTER XI

THE CEMETERY AND THE FARM HOUSE

The vivid dreams of the Civil War were beginning to appear less frequently now. While a dream of the Civil War was occurring about once every two weeks, it was now about once every two months. I tried to remain as ignorant of Civil War history as possible, ignoring the movie "Gettysburg" and resisting the urge to see any movies on TV that dealt with the Civil War. Although I was browsing through reference books from time to time in order to verify historical details of my dreams and answer my own questions, I refrained from reading any novels about the Civil War. I never knew when the dreams would finally end, and I didn't want my dreams to be influenced by what I read or saw in the movies.

The dreams I had experienced at this point left me still wondering who I was and where I was at the time of each dream. Everything was so clear to me concerning our encampment by that little town, and yet upon awakening, I hadn't the slightest clue as to where I was at that time. If I had listened to the ramblings of the young soldier as he sat under the tree talking to the other two men who were sitting with him, maybe I would have heard and remembered something from him when I awoke. As it was, I was too nervous and fidgety to concentrate on anything being said by anyone. I couldn't even sit and relax. I was too occupied pacing back and forth and watching for any attack from the Federal troops.

As the weeks went by and another month passed, I realized that my usual two week pattern had indeed been broken. By that time it had been almost two months before another unusual dream occurred. I believe this was once again a journey into the past, mainly due to the vivid details of this dream. There were no soldiers in uniform to contend with, but somehow I felt this dream was part of my past experience in the Civil War.

It was daylight with cloudy skies, and I was standing at the gate of a small cemetery. The fence was about 6 feet high and made of black wrought iron, twisted in a fancy design. The gate, as well as the beautifully engraved arch shaped sign above the gate, was also black wrought iron. I could see the word "Cemetery" engraved in the sign, with a row of swirls and roses etched above and below the word. The entire fenced in area was only about 30 by 40 feet.

I stood there looking through the tall wrought iron gate for a brief moment at the small monuments and headstones. For some reason I felt compelled to enter the cemetery. I knew the gate would be unlocked as I pushed it open. Something about the cemetery felt familiar, and the thought of trespassing never entered my mind as I began to walk among the headstones.

The cemetery was very small and seemed to be located out in the middle of nowhere. I would estimate the whole fenced in area to be no larger than the average person's front yard. It appeared to be very well kept, as the grass was cut, and even the wrought iron fence did not show any sign of paint peeling or rust. The art work on some of the small monuments was very impressive as well as a few large marble monuments, whose sculptured figurines almost rivaled that of Michaelangelo. The majority of the headstones were small and plain and appeared to be made of granite. Many had a light orange and beige swirl. Many of the small monuments were sculptured with crosses and religious designs.

I seemed to be looking for the names on the headstones and monuments as I made my way around them. As I focused my attention on each headstone, I couldn't seem to be able to read the names. The names must have been engraved on them somewhere, but perhaps the reason I don't remember the names is that I may have been looking for one name in particular, and the names of the people I didn't know left my thoughts as quickly as I read them. My dream ended with my wandering from headstone to headstone.

My waking observation was that this could have been a private cemetery of a very wealthy family. I don't recall seeing any houses nearby, but that's not to say there were none. My focus was mainly directed at the artistic architecture of the fence and the headstones and my search for the names. If it was a private family plot, the fence around it would prevent any further burials, as the cemetery was filled to capacity. The headstones were erected from fence to fence with barely enough room to walk around the headstones.

I was alone in this dream and I have no idea why I was there at that cemetery. The thought of that dream persisted for the next few days, and I wondered if I could find some old photos of wealthy old homes with the family cemetery plot nearby. These dreams leave such a vivid and haunting impression on my mind that I'm always searching for photos of the areas where the dream appeared to happen. I always feel the need to know where I was after the dream has ended.

A trip to the library had me scanning the history

section and a pictorial book of the Civil War caught my eye. As I sat browsing through the book an interesting photo captured my attention. It was an old photo of men and women visiting a cemetery that looked very much like the one in my dream, except the one in the photo was a group of small plots, each separated by a wrought iron fence. The photo was taken in 1863 in Lexington, Virginia and showed visitors paying their respects to the recently buried General Thomas "Stonewall" Jackson.

The cemetery in my dream was not a group of plots, but rather one small cemetery completely enclosed by a wrought iron fence. It was surrounded by a field with a small hill in the background, and a few trees scattered here and there. Perhaps I was looking for the final resting place of an officer slain in battle whom I served under, or maybe I was looking for the grave of a family loved one. I guess I'll never know.

THE FARM HOUSE

The following dream occurred some months later and was also one of a peaceful and serene nature. The dream began as I was walking out a door onto the porch of an old wooden farm house. On my right I could see what seemed to be an extended part of the house protruding out to the porch. Perhaps it was a shed or an addition built on to a room. It apparently had rained the night before, as the wooden porch appeared almost black, as wood often does when it is wet. I walked toward the porch railing to see what the weather was like and rested my right hand on the porch roof support beam. It was then that I noticed I was wearing a long sleeve buckskin shirt. The shirt appeared to be homemade and the sleeves were sewn on at the shoulders with thin strips of red leather.

As I stood there looking out at my land, the air was

cool and crisp. It must have been the Fall season, as the trees that grew in the woods on the other side of my split rail fence were sparse of foliage, but still adorned with some colorful leaves. Two tall thin trees stood conspicuously well above the other trees in the woods. They were growing side by side and had short branches, but for some unknown reason the top of the tree on the left was leaning considerably, as if a huge weight were attached to the top of it. As I looked to my right, I could see a small gold patch of wheat growing by my fence. I don't know whether the land I was looking at was the front of my house or the back. My property seemed to extend only about 100 feet from my porch. I couldn't see any road or path on the other side of the fence. It seemed to be only thick bushes and weeds along the edge of the woods.

As I stood there observing my surroundings, I took several deep breathes of that clear crisp air. It was so quiet and I seemed to be alone. I wasn't aware of anyone else nearby, but the dream didn't start until I had just stepped out onto the porch. I never got a chance to see the inside of my house, so it's possible I wasn't alone and had family living with me. After a minute or two I began to feel restless and figured I had better get started on my chores. As I turned around I saw a tall white metal milk urn setting on the porch under a window. I walked over to it and lifted it by the rimmed edge at the top and started to carry it around to the other side of the house. The porch extended past the side of the house allowing for a wooden walkway to the back of the house. At this moment I awoke.

Perhaps this brief moment of my previous life occurred before the Civil War began. I had no thoughts of war at all, only of my farm chores. I was very tall in this dream also, as my head was not far from the sloping porch roof. I may have been about 19 or 20 years of age, just before the Civil War had begun. This may have been my home in Roanoke, Virginia that I spoke of during my hypnosis session with Dr. Holzer. I haven't been there in this lifetime, but I have heard much of it is farmland.

I had apparently been given a temporary reprieve from the emotional anxiety that usually accompanies my dreams of trying to stay alive in battle. These two dreams were brief and uneventful but they often haunt my thoughts. Even though neither of these dreams seemed to have any direct involvement with the Civil War, I somehow felt as if I were living in that era of time. Just the fact that both dreams were so colorful and unforgettable seems to indicate they are a product of hypnosis. I enjoyed the dream of the farmhouse. The clarity of the scenery that appeared before me on that crisp Fall morning will always remain an indelible memory.

CHAPTER XII

THE CARNAGE

As the weeks went by it seemed like my temporary reprieve from dreams of battlefield action came to an end, for my most depressing dream was soon to follow. My dream began as I was lying on a field looking up at the clear blue sky. Apparently this must have been the aftermath of a violent battle, as I immediately became aware of lying in a tangled mass of dead soldiers. I made an attempt to move my arms and legs but realized I couldn't move. I didn't know whether I was paralyzed or just too exhausted to move.

I found I was able to raise my head, however, and as I looked down toward my feet I was shocked at the sight of a gaping round hole in my right pelvis. I did not see any blood but the threads in my gray trousers surrounding the wound were singed. I also could see the bodies of two soldiers lying across my legs. One was a Federal trooper who was lying face down across my knees. He was still wearing his blue hat. Perhaps he was the one who inflicted my wound. The other soldier was a Confederate who was lying on his right side across my ankles.

As I began to crane my neck to try to look around, I realized my shoulders were wedged against the bodies of other dead soldiers. I strained to see to my right over the dead soldier's body, and I couldn't believe what I saw. The field was huge and as far as the eye could see were bodies of dead and wounded soldiers lying in a entangled heap. On the distant horizon was a long plateau on which appeared a smaller plateau. As I turned to my left, I could see the back of a dead soldier who was lying on his left side and propped up against my left shoulder. His dirty wet gray jacket would indicate he was a Confederate. While turning my head around upward I could see a dead soldier wearing a blue cap whose head was almost touching mine. He had very prominent cheek bones and a long pointed nose. He also had a short black pointed beard.

It soon became evident that there were other survivors as the sound of wailing could be heard all across the field. As I lay there waiting for the voices of a medical or burial detail, the sun was rising higher in the sky. I was sweating profusely and wished I had fallen under the shade of the small tree that stood about 75 feet from me instead of here in the open field. There I would at least be shielded from the hot sun. I must have been lying there for hours, and as the sun lowered on the horizon the air became cooler, much to my relief. The vest I was wearing under my jacket that only compounded my problem with the heat soon became a comfort against the chill in the night air.

After the sun set I was watching the clear sky and it seemed like every star in the universe was visible that night. I knew I probably wouldn't last the night, and I lay there in disbelief and total despair that no one had come to help us. As I lay there watching the stars and listening to the awful cries and delirium of the wounded, I awoke.

This was possibly my final day of this previous lifetime.

I would like to think that we were not completely forsaken by our own men and that a medical unit or burial detail were at least dispatched to that field the next day. Perhaps there were no survivors to report back to request help for the rest of us. If I had somehow survived such a drastic wound, I'm sure my fighting days were at an end.

Unlike normal dreams that we all experience every night, the details of these dreams seem to become more clear with passing time. They are constantly passing through my thoughts every day, and it seems I can recall some of the minor details of these dream experiences that I never bothered to discuss before, such as a thin leather strap across my chest. I remember it had a slightly rusted buckle and the sides of the strap had frayed edges. Although I didn't want to look too closely at the wound in my right hip area, I could see the burnt fringed edges of cloth sticking up in a round circle in my gray trousers. I don't know what I was struck with, but I assume the large caliber ammo used at that time could inflict a sizeable hole.

It's strange that I don't recall feeling pain in my lower body, but yet I felt uncomfortable with the changing temperatures. I was sweating from the noonday sun, and actually felt cool when the sun set. I also recall the murmuring and moaning, and even the shouting from the delirious. Some of the things that were heard from the shouting really made no sense at all, and in fact would seem quite comical if they were spoken in a drunken revelry in a saloon instead of mindless delirium on a battlefield.

When I realize that the mass of tangled bodies were both Federal and Confederate soldiers, I must assume there must have been a lot of hand to hand combat. I wasn't aware of any sign of life in the soldiers who were lying so close to me. However, all of the moaning and hollering across the field indicated at that time there were many survivors. How many of us made it through the night I'll never know.

Since this dream began with the aftermath of a battle, I don't have any recollection of actually engaging in combat with the Federal troops. Perhaps the battle began early in the morning and lasted only a few hours, as the sun was still high in the sky when the dream began. My knowledge of the famous battles of the Civil War is almost nonexistent, but perhaps if I were a Civil War buff, I would recognize the terrain around me and be able to identify the area in which this battle took place. My view of the whole field was restricted, of course, since I could only raise my head enough to see over the bodies that lay around me. Perhaps that unusual landmark of the long plateau on which another small plateau appeared would be a clue. The only other landmark I could see was that small tree, which didn't seem out of the ordinary.

Since I actually felt no pain, either my wound was superficial or maybe I was paralyzed. It's quite possible I was simply immobilized due to all the weight on and against me from the bodies of those dead soldiers, but I don't recall putting much effort into even trying to move my arms or legs. Even with the bodies of the two soldiers lying across them, I'm sure I could have managed to pull my legs out from under them. I did feel completely exhausted, and with my concern for my wound, I may have felt it best not to even try to move my body. It was an effort just to lift my head and try to look around. I don't recall being injured in my other past life dreams of the Civil War, but perhaps the absence of pain in a past life dream experience is a blessing for which one should be grateful.

This wasn't the first dream of putting my life in danger in battle, but was it my last? I don't know if these dreams were being presented to me in a chronological order of past events or simply sporadic fragmented memories. My thoughts as I lay on that field were more of disappointment and even betrayal. So many of us gave such a sacrifice for our cause and just when we needed help we lay abandoned. I'm sure help came eventually, but we were sprawled far and wide across that field for so long, I feared that we would never be found more than I feared death.

CHAPTER XIII

MY PEN PAL

Month after month had gone by without another dream of the Civil War. Many nights I would see if I could induce another dream of my Civil War experiences by trying to suggest to myself that I would have another dream of the Civil War. I would lay there at night when I knew I was ready to doze off and repeat over and over in my mind that another such dream would occur, but these attempts were never successful. It just wasn't something I could turn on and off or control in any way.

When I visited Dr. Holzer that day, I was hoping for a complete hypnotic regression. Everything I have ever read of the successful regressions resulted in the subject being completely submerged in another time and place of history. They are usually oblivious to their present surroundings and can recall with complete clarity such personal matters as their name, age, date of birth as well as their place of birth in that past life. They can usually describe exactly what they are doing at that particular moment as well as what is going on around them. If they were someone of some social or political prominence from the past, sometimes verification of other personal information can be made if enough research material is available on this person.

More often though the subject of hypnotic regression

is an obscure person who has made little if any impact on history. Aside from the strange feeling of reliving the whole dream experience of the skirmish in the woods in my mind, I had some doubts that anything more would come of it. In spite of the fact that I was a little disappointed at first of the results of our hypnotic session that day, I was more than satisfied at the final results many months later.

As the months went by the dreams of the Civil War seemed to have ended, but those dreams I experienced over those months have never left me. They are in my thoughts every day although I am not troubled by them. Since the dreams and flashbacks appeared to have ended, I was still left with a feeling of curiosity as to who I really was in that period of time. I find it a little fascinating that even though I was unable to attain total hypnotic regression, my previous life was shown to me over a period of time in bits and pieces. Each piece seemed to have an important purpose to assemble the whole puzzle.

I don't really know at this point the actual chronology of events as they appeared to me over the months since I met Dr. Holzer, and of course the two dreams I had some 24 Years ago. I don't know if I lived to see the end of the Civil War. I was in a precarious situation several times, but none so hopeless as the dream of being so severely wounded on a field of dead and wounded soldiers.

The research I had done when the dreams ended was very fruitful, as so many of the little details that I remembered so well were factually authenticated. Even though names and places were not mentioned up to this point in these dream experiences, it was the little details such as clothing and military equipment that I was able to verify through a lot of research that convinces me, as well as Dr. Holzer, that this was evidence enough of a past life memory. I wrote to the Virginia State Library and Archives in Richmond and requested any information they might have on file of a Sgt. Albert Richardson. Of course, I didn't tell them the reason for my inquiry. They told me that the information I requested is not available from the Archives Branch, and suggested that I send my request to the National Archives in Washington, D.C. I received no information from them on this request.

I recently discovered a Albert Richardson listed in a Who's Who book of the Civil War. He was a New York war correspondent who, during his news coverage of the war, was captured by the Confederates. He spent many months in a prisoner of war camp before finally escaping back to New York. Apparently, his name was probably as popular to the North and the South during the Civil War, just as war correspondent Ernie Pyle was during World War II. Maybe it was his name that came to mind during the hypnosis session if he was so well known at that time. While reading my June 1995 issue of Fate Magazine one day, I came across a feature called, "Reader of the Month." The article highlights a reader's interests and hobbies, and an explanation of why Fate is such a favorite magazine to them. In this particular issue a woman from Salt Lake City, Utah was profiled. Her name was Kristin Burton, and she explained why she reads Fate, and asked any readers who shared her interests in ghosts, reincarnation, etc. to write to her. She mentioned that living in a Mormon community, she has no one to discuss and share her interests in these topics. I immediately wrote to her and we have been pen pals ever since. I told her I too have no one to share these unusual dream experiences, as for the most part, my family and friends seem to have no interest in these subjects, if not completely skeptical.

During our correspondence, I sent to Kristin a copy of a manuscript I had typewritten of my whole experience with all of these dreams of the Civil War up to that point, as well as my hypnotic session with Dr. Holzer. We continued to share our unusual experiences during our correspondence, and have occasionally recommended reading material of the paranormal variety to each other. Her interests have also made her a fan of Hans Holzer's books, and we both agreed that his book, *Life Beyond* was one of his best in dealing with reincarnation.

Dr. Holzer stated that religious philosophy played absolutely no part in his work, and that the purpose of his book was to determine by analysis whether reincarnation is a fact or fallacy. His description of the many views on the process of the soul being reborn in many countries throughout the world was interesting. For example, in Africa it is believed the soul returns into the bodies of their descendants, such as the souls of important warriors or kings return in the bodies of their children.

I also found interesting his two chapters on the scientific view and the religious view of reincarnation. Dr. Holzer relates in the former chapter of the belief and research in reincarnation of Dr. Ian Stevenson, who is head of the Department of Neurology and Psychiatry at the University of Virginia's School of Medicine. Although his research has provided much evidence to support his theory of reincarnation, he has difficulty in finding acceptance from orthodox scientists who believe that only laboratory experiments can prove the existence of reincarnation. At this time, no one has been able to think of a way to conduct a test in a laboratory to prove or disprove his theory.

Dr. Holzer also mentions that some support for reincarnation research can be found among physical scientists because in learning about the nature of energy and mass and in dealing with the electromagnetic force in the universe, they have come to realize that energy is indestructible. They feel that energy can never be dissipated entirely, and since the human personality is an energy field, it cannot be dissipated either and must therefore continue to exist in some form. He also mentioned that medical science has been more hostile toward reincarnation material than any other branch of science, possibly because they rely heavily upon the assumption that a person is essentially a physical being.

Dr. Holzer's chapter on the religious view of reincarnation was also very interesting and informative. He states that the religious establishment has viewed reincarnation with various attitudes. The early days of Christianity seem to have suggested reincarnation, but this concept was later discouraged by the church, and many material that referred to it was deleted in later texts. Throughout this chapter it seems to be a common consensus in the Western regions that reincarnation, with the exception of a few modern churches, is not acceptable.

For the reader who is interested in more than the philosophy of reincarnation, Dr. Holzer's book also has several chapters on some of the people he has hypnotically regressed. While under hypnosis these people gave such incredible detailed information about their past lives that this book held my interest from cover to cover. Although I haven't read all of Dr. Holzer's books, I'm sure this had to be one of his best.

I found my correspondence with Kristin to be very exciting and always looked forward to her next letter. It was such a comfort to finally be able to talk about some of the unusual experiences I have had over the years. She expressed an interest in the detailed journal I had sent to her concerning my dreams of the Civil War up to this point and offered to assist in the research to try to verify the existence of Albert Richardson. She said she spoke with a friend who is not only very knowledgeable about Civil War history, but is also an avid genealogist.

Her friend told her that requesting information from the Archives in Washington, D.C. can take a long time, and a lot more information on Union soldiers can be found there than on Confederate soldiers. She also discovered from her friend that the genealogical library in Salt Lake City has extensive records regarding Confederate soldiers. This was a surprise to me, as I never associated Utah with having anything to do with the Civil War, especially to the point of keeping records of those who served in the war. Although I was not sure of my past life identity, this name entered my thoughts during the hypnosis for a reason. I didn't want to put Krisitn through a lot of trouble spending a lot of time going through endless records and possibly all for nothing, but she seemed enthusiastic and very interested in the project. I thanked her and told her I would certainly appreciate any information she could find.

In one of her letters, Kristin asked me if I would be interested in trying out an audio tape of self-hypnosis she had recently purchased. She said it may help jog my memory with another dream or flashback. It had been a long time since I had my last dream experience of the Civil War. However, since I didn't seem to be susceptible to deep hypnosis while under the instruction of a professional hypnotist, I just couldn't put too much enthusiasm on a self-instruction audio tape. Even though I would listen to it while no one was around, I probably would feel a little silly. I thought concentration would also be a problem, as the mind has a tendency to wander if the interest is lacking. After giving it some thought, I wrote back to her and told her I would try her self-hypnosis tape. After all, what did I have to lose? I had never heard any of these audio self-instruction tapes and it would be kind of interesting to hear what they are like. I thought it was quite generous of Kristin to make a duplicate tape and mail it to me.

A few weeks later I received the tape in the mail. I picked an evening when I would be alone and free of any distractions and got comfortable on my couch with my portable tape recorder by my side. As the tape began I followed the instructions of the melodious voice of the instructor. The soothing voice gave the usual suggestions of gradual total relaxation and mental imagery. The instructions were accompanied by the weirdest background music I have ever heard.

As I focused my attention on the voice of the instructor I was surprised to find I was indeed feeling very relaxed. In fact, I felt so relaxed while listening to the tape, I even had a little concern of getting too comfortable, and perhaps become a semi-conscious victim of my own self-hypnosis. When the tape ended about 30 minutes later, I had not experienced any dreams or mental images of the Civil War during the playing of the tape. It was nothing more than a relaxing experience. I left the tape in the recorder with the intention of giving it another try sometime soon.

CHAPTER XIV

THE GENERAL

Several nights after I listened to the self-hypnosis tape sent to me by Kristin, I had another vivid dream of the Civil War. Since the dream did not occur while I was listening to the tape or even that same night, I don't really know if the tape was responsible for the dream. I suppose it could have been just a delayed reaction. I was going to pass this dream experience off as just an ordinary dream due to the unusual circumstances, and some of the details required some explanation. However, as the days went by I couldn't get the dream out of my mind. It stuck with me just as all the other dreams of the Civil War have done, and gradually some of the questionable details of the dream began to make sense. Here then, is the dream that had a few surprises in store for me.

The dream began as we were on the losing end of a battle on a large field surrounded by woods. It was a beautiful Spring day with a clear blue sky. A few puffy white clouds could be seen scattered across the sky. I found myself running across a field with several other Confederate soldiers with both hands firmly gripping my rifle which I carried in front of me. At that moment I don't know whether I was the pursued or the pursuer, as I don't recall any fear or heightened anxiety. Perhaps we were running toward a better battle position in the field.

As I approached a small tree with its low gnarled branches spread out, I saw our commanding officer picking himself up from the ground. When he made it to his feet I could see that he was a general, although his disheveled gray uniform was covered with dry brown dirt. I ran past him but stopped about 20 feet away and as I turned to face him I noticed he seemed to be in trouble. I watched as he struggled to maintain his balance, and I could see he had a problem with his left leg. Although I could see no blood I could tell he was wounded below the left knee. He wore shin high boots but the left trouser leg seemed to be almost flat, giving the impression his left leg was badly damaged below the knee. As he tried to keep his balance his left leg seemed to almost buckle under him. Since I could see no blood, perhaps this was a problem for him as a result of a previous injury.

My concern for the general had my attention focused on him and I could see that his pale blue eyes appeared to be dazed. As he continued to sway and stagger he looked disoriented but still defiant. He may have just fallen from his horse, as he tried to stand and fight. He was standing near a small tree with low spread out gnarled branches. Perhaps he didn't see a low branch and was knocked off his horse. He was a man of average stature with a rather thin build. He looked to be in his late forties, as his thick reddish brown hair and well groomed pointed beard were streaked with gray. In his dazed condition he was trying to put on his hat, but it was a strange looking hat. It wasn't the usual round rimmed "cowboy hat" or the flat top cap with a peak. His hat was long and flat with a curved design cut in the front, very much like the kind worn by Napoleon Bonaparte. As he stood there trying to keep his balance, I felt very concerned for the "old man."

As I stood watching the general and trying to decide if he needed my help, I could see a whole company of Federal troops emerging from the distant woods from which we had just come. The general couldn't see them coming since he was facing me. I knew I couldn't leave the general alone, as he looked so disoriented and helpless. He couldn't even run very well with that bad leg. I watched as the Federal troops got closer carrying their rifles at waist level, as if in a "fixed bayonet" charge position. It seemed as if they were so young and as they quickly approached us I could see the grin on some of their faces.

I didn't know how "trigger happy" these young troops would be and I knew we were just sitting ducks. I was aware that the general was unarmed, as he was not carrying his rifle, and his holster for his service revolver was empty. Even his sword was gone. Perhaps he lost everything when he may have fallen from his horse. As the Federal troops were closing in on us, I hollered out to the general, "Sam, surrender! You have nothing left to fight with!" At that moment I felt the hard barrel of a rifle being pushed into my back. I tossed my rifle down to the ground and raised my arms over my head. I had the urge to turn around but thought better of that idea. There is nothing like the feel of the hard steel barrel of a rifle being shoved into your back to put you in a mood of compliance.

I watched the general as I stood there with my arms in the air. He was making me nervous because he still had not raised his hands in surrender. He still didn't seem to comprehend the situation, as he stood there swaying with a defiant look in his eye. As four young Federal troopers approached him, he finally raised his hands in a brief gesture of surrender. I watched the expression on the faces of the four young Federal troopers as they approached the general. They were smiling as they grabbed his arms, probably because they got themselves a general, I thought to myself. As the Federal trooper pushed the barrel of his rifle into my back he ordered me to walk. Satisfied that the general would not be harmed,

"As I stood watching the general and trying to decide if he needed my help, I could see a whole company of Federal troops emerging from the distant woods from which we had just came."

I walked toward the woods with my arms in the air. Before I took more than a few steps, I awoke.

This dream made quite an impression on me. It was as vivid and colorful as my other dreams of the Civil War, but I had lingering doubts about this experience being a past life memory due to a few minor details, such as my familiarity with the general. Nevertheless, it haunted my thoughts constantly. I couldn't get the image of that general standing by that tree and struggling to keep his balance out of my mind.

About a week or two after this dream I was once again browsing in the bookstore at the mall. While scanning the shelves in the history department I spotted a book I had never noticed before. It was entitled, *Generals in Gray* by Ezra J. Warner. It was a thick book and listed most if not all the generals in the Confederate Army from A to Z. I had no idea there were so many Confederate generals in the Civil War. As I scanned through the book to see how many generals were named Sam, I was shocked when I came across a photo of General Samuel McGowan. As I stared at the photo in disbelief, I had no doubt that this was the man in my dream, pointed beard and all. The information on each general was very brief, but it mentioned he was a general of the Army of Northern Virginia, and was wounded in four different battles, but it didn't mention how he was wounded or the extent of his injuries. He was born in 1819 and lived well past the Civil War, having died in 1897.

About a week after my dream of General McGowan, I wrote to my pen pal, Kristin, and explained to her in every detail the adventures in my latest dream. Several details of the dream made me doubtful at first if this could have been a past life memory. The most unusual detail was that I called my commanding general by his first name. I should have addressed him as General

McGowan or Sir, but certainly not Sam. Perhaps my concern for his safety made me forget military protocol for a minute, or possibly he had such a personal rapport with the men that titles were often relaxed. This was the first time in all of my dreams of the Civil War that I can remember calling out a name. I thought it was interesting to note that I thought of the general as a "father" figure, when in this life and at the time of the dream. I was probably about 10 years older than the general was at his time in the Civil War.

Another detail of the dream that left me with doubts was that it didn't seem to correspond with my dream of the carnage. If I were taken prisoner on the field that day, how did I end up lying on a field of dead and wounded soldiers with a big hole in my hip? Since these dreams were probably not in chronological order, either I may have survived the carnage and was able to fight again, or I escaped my captors when the general and I surrendered. Perhaps our captivity was very brief, as the tide can turn in a battle from one hour to the next.

One other detail in that dream left me with doubts when I awoke. It was the unusual hat the general was trying to put on his head. It seemed to be more from the Napoleonic Army than the Confederate Army, and yet I remember that the shade of gray of the hat was a perfect match of his gray uniform. I didn't think anything of his hat at the time of the dream, but I realized when I awoke it didn't seem to match the uniforms of that time.

While browsing through a Civil War book of antiques several months later, I was surprised to see a picture of the hat the general wore in that dream. It was called a chapeau, and they were not only worn during the Civil War, they were U.S. Government issued. By this I am assuming they were issued to the Federal troops, and perhaps the general came across it during the aftermath of a battle and had it dyed to match his uniform. While not having all the answers to the unusual events taking place during these dreams of the Civil War, at least I was finding information that substantiated some of the historical details.

Satisfied that this could have been another past life memory of the Civil War, I wrote to Hans Holzer and explained the dream in full detail. I told him I could not find much information on General McGowan at the library, and the book of Confederate Generals had only a brief biography. I told him about my Pen pal and that we were both going to continue to seek out any other information we could find about him. I particularly wanted to know if he was ever wounded below the left knee and if he was ever taken prisoner during one of his battles, even for a brief time.

It seemed my attention was so focused on the general during that dream, I don't remember much of what was going on around me. I was so worried about the general I didn't even know a Federal trooper was coming up behind me. When he poked that rifle barrel in my back, I didn't dare turn around. My cooperation probably saved me from getting shot, even though I really did want to look at my captor. Even though I was only about 24 years of age in this dream, the Federal troopers who walked up to the general and grabbed his arms looked so young to me. They may have been only in their late teens. I'll never forget the smiles on their faces as they started to take the general away. It seems my captor sensed my personal concern for the general, and he waited until I could see that he would not be hurt and would be treated with dignity. It wasn't until then that he pushed the barrel of his rifle into my back and told me to walk. The command to "walk" was the only word I heard him say.

This dream had been an exciting and interesting experience for me, but I was unprepared for the fascinating chain of events that was soon to follow.

CHAPTER XV

THE INCREDIBLE COINCIDENCE

About a week after I wrote to Dr. Holzer about my dream of the general I received a package from him in the mail. Since my last letter to him concerned my dream of General McGowan, I thought it may be a reference book of the Civil War, with information about the general in particular. As I opened the package, much to my surprise it contained his book entitled, *Great American Ghost Stories*. There was no letter or even a brief note to explain his sending me a book of ghost stories, but I was happy to receive it nevertheless. Reading about his exploits and investigations with troubled departed spirits with the help of a medium has made me such a fan of his writings for so many years.

I quickly noticed a small blank piece of paper marking a chapter called, "The Fifth Avenue Ghost." I assumed he wanted me to read that chapter in particular so I began to read, still assuming the book, and particularly a chapter about a haunting in New York City, had nothing to do with General McGowan, or even the Civil War for that matter.

As I became engrossed in his story of the ghost who was haunting an apartment in New York City, I realized about half way through the story why Dr. Holzer had sent this book to me. In a seance with a medium and a group of researchers, Dr. Holzer was able to make contact with and interview the troubled spirit. Dr. Holzer wrote that the spirit was reluctant to identify himself, but in a series of 17 seance sessions that lasted over a period of 5 months, which began in July 1953 through November of that year, the spirit finally identified himself as General Samuel McGowan.

Throughout each interview with McGowan, with the assistance of a medium, it became apparent his memory was better at describing scenes from his life rather than names and dates. He could recall and describe his participation in battle, but he was hazy in trying to remember his own date of birth. I can relate to this myself, as I can recall with such clarity the skirmish in the woods, but I don't know where I was or wasn't even sure of my own name. When Dr. Holzer asked him what he did at the end of the war, he replied his property was ruined and his house burned, and he moved to New York City. At one time during a seance, Dr. Holzer questioned McGowan about landmarks and business proprietors at the time of his residence there. When Dr. Holzer later did some research to verify the accuracy of McGowan's answers, he found them quite accurate down to the last detail. His memory of Victorian expressions of that time period and even the name of the mayor of New York City was right on target. I got the impression from reading this chapter of Dr. Holzer's book that General McGowan must have enjoyed living in New York City. Apparently, he had no problem remembering the pleasant details of his life.

There is also mention of information about Samuel McGowan's military career in this chapter, derived from a book by J.F.J. Caldwell in 1866. One of the quotations that impressed me was, "General McGowan returned to us in February (1864). He had not sufficiently recovered from the wound received at Chancellorsville to walk well but remained with us and discharged all the duties of his office." This information is consistent with my dream of his unstable balance on the field and his wounded left leg below the knee.

I wrote back to Dr. Holzer to thank him for sending the book. I also pointed out how incredible this whole coincidence was, and it was also amazing to me that he remembered exactly where to find this article in his vast collection of books, especially since this interview during the seance took place in 1953, over 40 years ago. It seems General McGowan touched both of our lives, even so many years after his death. My dream encounter with General McGowan occurred about 40 years after his spirit interview with Dr. Holzer, and yet fate has brought Dr. Holzer and myself together to share this strange experience. I couldn't have been more surprised when I read of Dr. Holzer's interview of the spirit of a man who had just appeared so vividly to me in a dream. It almost seems as if Sam McGowan wants to emerge once again.

In spite of General McGowan's spirit mentioning some of his hardships and battles during the interviews with Dr. Holzer, I was still wondering about his wounds, and if he suffered any damage to his left leg below the knee. I also wondered about our capture on the field that day. I still needed some confirmation to convince myself that this wasn't just a dream, in spite of all the evidence that suggested otherwise. The absence of blood on his lower left leg may have been an indication he was just favoring a bad leg from a previous wound. Another theory could be that these past life memories were shown to me with some of the gory details eliminated from my subconscious. An example of seeing a wound without the blood is the dream of my lying on that field of dead and wounded soldiers. I could see that large round hole in my trousers, even to the point of remembering the singed threads surrounding the hole. Although I didn't want to dwell on my wound for fear of becoming nauseated, I don't recall seeing any blood.

There was also the capture and surrender of General McGowan and myself. In all the reference books I browsed through there was little information on General McGowan, only the historical text book timetable of the dates of his war promotions and the battles he served in. This may have been only a brief battlefield incident that didn't last long enough to warrant mention in the history books, as conditions and circumstances can change in minutes.

When Dr. Holzer asked McGowan about his personal appearance during his prime, his description was consistent with my impression of him in my dream. Through the medium's control spirit, he was described as slight of build and about 5'9" or 5'10" tall. McGowan's spirit also described himself as he looked in his prime. He said, "He had a very good brow, face to the long, and at one time I indulged in the whiskers, though not so long for the chin. I liked to see my chin a good deal." In my dream he wore a very short pointed beard with a mustache and had a very high forehead. He would probably have been about 5'10" tall and he was thin. Since I was well over 6 feet tall, I had to look down at him and he did appear thin, as his uniform even seemed a little too large for him. His eyes appeared to be pale blue and his reddish brown hair was streaked with gray. Since the only photo I have ever seen of General McGowan was an old black and white from the neck up, I wouldn't have had any way of knowing what his body weight and height would have been. I wouldn't have even seen his photo in that book of Confederate Generals if I hadn't scanned through that book long after that dream occurred.

In order to verify this information and convince myself once and for all about his physical appearance and his wounds suffered during four battles of the Civil War, I wrote to the National Archives and Records Administration in Washington D.C. and requested a copy of General Samuel McGowan's military record, as well as any documents that would indicate his physical description and his medical records. A few weeks after I sent my request to the National Archives, I received a form from them to fill out and return. Thanks to the book Dr. Holzer sent to me, I was able to supply all the information requested on the form, such as the Unit in which he served, date and place of birth and death, and even places he lived after his military service. I was even able to supply the name of his widow, of course now deceased, but I thought the more personal information I was able to supply, the faster they could find and send the information I requested.

I had never heard of General Samuel McGowan before the research of my dream, and now I was engrossed in his military as well as his personal life. The instructions on the form from the Archives recommended requesting a copy of the pension files of the subject of the search, rather than the military service record. However, since I am only interested in General McGowan's physical description and his military medical records, I requested a copy of his military service record. The fact that he was a Confederate soldier probably would have made him ineligible for a government pension. Anyway, the information contained in a pension file would likely be of more interest to someone who is trying to trace a veteran's genealogy.

It seems just when I think the dreams of the Civil War have come to an end, I have another dream that is too vivid to ignore. This one was so brief that I was not going to mention it, but just as all of these dreams seem to have a lingering effect, this one appears to be no exception.

I seemed to be observing a camp of Federal troops in a large clearing from my position in the woods. It looked like a mass of blue uniforms, as there seemed to be about 150 Federal troops milling about. They didn't seem to be carrying their rifles, so I guess they were just trying to relax and set up camp. It seemed to be late in the day, as the sky was a little hazy and the sun was low. I was lying on my stomach in the high weeds and thick underbrush, and the fact that my point of observation was on a hill also gave me some reassurance that I wouldn't be seen.

I don't know where they were returning from but there were some rowdies in the group. I doubt if they had just returned from a battle, as they seemed too full of energy. Suddenly, a fist fight broke out among a rather large group of troops, as the troops on the outer edge of the group seemed to be turning and directing their punches inward toward the center of the group. Soon a big brawl ensued. I couldn't see whether they were punching one or two persons in particular, perhaps prisoners for example, or perhaps they were just getting on each other's nerves. My dream was so brief, but they were still brawling when I awoke. I imagine the officers broke up the fight shortly thereafter. I don't know whether I was part of a company of Confederates waiting for dark to attack, or whether I was alone and just happened to come across the Federal camp while walking in the woods. If they were so keyed up to fight among themselves, it's fortunate they didn't see me.

One other dream I had about a week later pertaining to the Civil War was also brief, but reflected the modern changes in our weapons. I was crouched down in the high weeds on top of a hill on a bright sunny day. In front of me was a field overgrown with shrubs and weeds. On my right was a dense wooded area. I was alone and not a sound was heard from anywhere. I was busy loading my rifle, but it wasn't anything like my old one with the minnie balls and ramrod.

My rifle lay flat at my feet while I loaded bullets in an exposed chamber on the side of the rifle. The bullets were very strange in that they had a small gray pleated sack attached to them. The sack was about 1" and hung on the end of each bullet. As I said, the dream was brief and I awoke while loading these strange looking bullets into my rifle. I don't know what I was doing there all by myself. Why was I hiding in the tall weeds when there didn't seem to be anyone else around? Since I was on a hilltop, maybe I was a sniper waiting for someone to pass by on horseback. I had a good view of the field and also the edge of the woods.

When I awoke, I thought of how silly those bullets seem to look. The little sack attached to them felt coarse to the touch. I wasn't going to record this episode because it didn't make much sense to me, but I had a surprise coming several months later. At one of our local Civil War re-enactments at the park, tents and merchandise stands are located at the entrance to the Park. Some of the tables displayed old articles used at the time of the Civil War. I was shocked when I saw among the artifacts three bullets with the little sacks attached. I learned later that the sacks contained gunpowder, although it is still unclear to me how the bullet is propelled. Since I thought the details of this dream were too ridiculous to have been historically factual, I have been once again proven wrong. I decided to include this brief but enlightening dream experience.

Apparently, the dreams of the Civil War seemed to be continuing. At this point, it had been about two and a half years since my visit with Dr. Holzer for our hypnosis session. These dreams came to me often after the hypnosis, but slowly dwindled to one every several months. By this time I had assumed I would not have any more dreams, but perhaps they will continue for the rest of my life. However, I find these dreams of the past a fascinating experience rather than a troublesome one.

CHAPTER XVI

MY OTHER PAST LIVES

During my correspondence with my pen pal, Kristin, she asked me if I have ever experienced any other past life dreams besides the Confederate solder. I replied that I had three other vivid unforgettable dreams of living in another time, and although the dreams were only a one time experience, they still "haunt" me quite frequently.

About 16 years ago in 1986 1 dreamed I was a merchant in ancient Greece. My dream began as I stood in front of my open tent which displayed gold jewelry and ornaments of different sizes. I sold wrist bands, necklaces and various gold jewelry that glistened in the morning sun. On my left were big beautiful green rolling hills beyond which the sun rose every morning. Somehow, I felt I was about 28 years old and married with two sons, even though they were not in the dream. Thoughts of a pretty petite young woman with big light brown eyes and light brown hair flowing over her shoulders in ringlets ran through my mind. Also, two small bare footed boys with chunky legs and wild bushy blond hair running around the field passed through my thoughts. I felt very happy and content.

As I stood in front of my tent I could see two men in the distance wearing white tunics walking briskly shoulder to shoulder over a hill. As they got closer, I could see they each carried a very long spear in an upright position and close to their bodies. They appeared tall, and marched like soldiers in unison with their heads held high. When they got closer it was obvious they were coming to see me. When they approached me. I was shocked when they informed me I was under arrest. As they stood by my sides, each guard grabbed one of my upper arms and escorted me away.

I soon found myself in what appeared to be a makeshift courtroom that actually looked more like a large cave. The room was dimly illuminated with torches mounted on the stone walls. As I stood there in my white tunic and sandals between the two guards, they seemed to tower over me. With the guards still holding my arms I stood between them facing a magistrate who sat in a high back wooden chair at the end of a long wooden table. He appeared to be about 40 years old, short and mostly bald. His skin appeared to have a yellow tint, but perhaps the flames of the wall torches gave his skin this impression. On both sides of the magistrate stood a tunic attired guard, holding a long spear with the end of the shaft resting on the ground. They stood up straight with their eyes focused ahead of them.

As the magistrate stood up from his chair he held up a scroll and began reading the charges against me. It didn't take long to realize I was being arrested for not paying my taxes, and I was going to be imprisoned for a long time. As I stood there pondering my fate, I had a plan to prevent such a long incarceration by choosing suicide. I broke free from the guards who were holding my arms and jumped up on the table. I lunged at the magistrate with my arms outstretched as if to choke him. I assumed one of his guards would react quickly and pierce my heart with his spear. Instead, the guard on his right grabbed me and spun me around. As he did so, he pulled the shaft of his spear tightly against my throat. At this moment I awoke. I never had this dream again.

Since my knowledge of European history was as inept as Civil War history, one detail of this dream left me some doubt about its historical accuracy, and if it were indeed a past life memory. The fact that I was being arrested for not paying my taxes seemed a little strange to me when I awoke and thought about the dream. I have read that the American people began paying some kind of taxes at the beginning of the Civil War. It was imposed by President Lincoln to finance the cost of the war. I also read that the Federal income tax began just before the beginning of World War I. However, this dream took place in the most primitive times of civilization, and I seriously doubted anyone was paying taxes to any government.

Much to my surprise, I happened to come across some information concerning the paying of taxes and discovered that ancient Greece was indeed one of the first civilized nations to impose a tax on its citizens. When I think back to that dream after all these years, I'm surprised that I can still recall so many details, such as the walls of the courtroom. I still don't know if they were actually made of stone or this whole legal procedure took place in a cave. The torches mounted on the wall seemed to be about 10 feet apart, and there seemed to be enough light in the room. I can recall the high back wooden chair the magistrate sat on was etched with decorative carvings.

I had no real intention of harming the magistrate, but I wanted his guards to think so and to kill me instantly, rather than serve such a long time in prison. Since I awoke as soon as the guard pulled his spear shaft against my throat, I won't know whether I succeeded. Perhaps he was only restraining me and I spent the rest of that past life in prison. This dream occurred long before I read the book by Dr. Holzer, *The Psychic Side of*

Dreams, so I just assumed at the time it was nothing more than an unusual dream. However, just the fact that I can still remember every detail and it still pervades my thoughts, indicates it was more than just a dream.

Another dream which found me in another place and time was of riding in what seemed to be a military procession through a medieval town. I was riding on a big white horse with black spots on his neck and right shoulder. They looked like ink spots shaken from a fountain pen onto a white sheet of paper. It was a long procession of soldiers on horseback, wagons and various carts, all traveling at a walking pace. I glanced behind me and could see no end to this procession. In front of me was a big wooden buckboard type of wagon with a wooden cage seated on the floor near the back of the wagon. The cage was about 5 feet high and 5 feet wide, and was empty at the time. Perhaps it was used to hold chickens or small livestock.

We traveled past the white concrete and stone buildings which were adorned with colorful awnings. Suddenly, the townspeople emerged from their homes and shops shouting and gesturing menacingly. I remember one person in particular. He was a toothless and emaciated looking little old man with a stubbly beard and rounded shoulders. He was dressed in what appeared to be green leotards and a green stocking like cap on his head. He stood defiantly, scowling and shaking his clenched fist at me.

I don't know if we were part of an occupation force, or what our business was in that village, but we were surely not welcome. I somehow knew that the order was to keep moving and avoid any confrontation with the town people. While being nervously aware of the scurrying of the people in the street and hearing the angry shouts, I tried to maintain my composure by sitting up straight on my horse and keeping my eyes straight ahead. At this moment I awoke. This dream also occurred quite a few years ago and was never repeated.

As with the dream of ancient Greece, this dream also invades my thoughts quite often. I can recall some of the townspeople in my dream, even though I was trying to sit up straight on my horse and keep my eyes focused ahead to avoid any eye contact that may be misinterpreted as provocation. That little old man seemed to be the most upset and menacing to me, even though he didn't carry a weapon. It seemed the street became crowded with people in no time. Perhaps this was one reason we traveled so slowly.

I can also recall a large young woman with a long brown skirt that spread out like a bell. She was wearing a white apron that covered the front of her baggy sleeved blouse and all the way down to the bottom of her skirt. She crossed the street in front of the wooden cart in front of me. When she got to the other side of the street, she joined the crowd in jeering at us.

I can't recall what was on the left side of the street, but to my right seemed to be a continuous row of white concrete buildings, with people standing in the doorways shaking their fists at us. Perhaps they were shops or businesses as well as dwellings, as some of them were four stories high. The beautiful and brightly colored awnings that shaded the windows seems to stick in my mind.

I have no idea what country I was in, but the weather on that particular day was pleasant. No one seemed to be wearing any heavy outer garments. If the color of that little old man's outfit could be any indication, we may have been in Ireland. Where ever we were that day, I do know I was anxious to leave that village as soon as possible.

The third past life dream was very brief, but it was one of those rare times I got to see what I looked like. The dream began as I walked through the swinging doors of a saloon while carrying a huge antique rifle. I walked up to the bar and lay my rifle on the counter and ordered a drink. As I stared down at the beverage in my glass, I was aware of a petite young Indian woman standing several feet behind me. Although I was ignoring her I knew she was of the Paiute tribe and that she was my wife. She didn't speak a word, but waited patiently for me to finish my drink. She stood there silently with her head bowed.

Slowly, I looked up and saw a large mirror with a fancy brass frame hanging on the wall behind the bar. Although the saloon was rather dark I could see my reflection in the mirror. I appeared to be rather short but powerfully built. I had very broad shoulders and a large protruding jaw was evident beneath the shadow of my hat. I was wearing a gray and white checkered wool jacket. When I looked down at the bar I could see that my hands appeared to be very large and strong. I guess I had to be strong just to carry that big rifle around with me. I probably used it for hunting.

As I finished my drink, I turned to go out those swinging doors and saw that my wife was still waiting for me. She stood in the same spot several feet behind me with her head bowed. Somehow I knew in my dream that she was a Paiute Indian, even though when I awoke, I never heard of that tribe. I had to do a little research to verify the existence of such a tribe. She never spoke to me but followed me around like a servant, with her head bowed and always remaining about 5 feet behind me. She was actually quite pretty and very young, and was wrapped in a blanket or shroud of some sort. I had a waking impression that I probably didn't deserve such a nice young woman.

This dream took place in the daytime, as the bright sunshine seemed to help illuminate the darkness of the saloon. I don't remember if there were any other customers in the saloon as I walked right up to the bar and must have ordered a drink, although I don't recall what the bartender looked like. It seems that I didn't pay much attention to my surroundings. In fact, I kept my head down most of the time. I was looking at my glass and at my huge rifle, which seemed like an antique even for those times. The brass stock plate and trigger guard had a very fancy intricate design. Perhaps it was an heirloom, as I seemed to take such pride in that old rifle.

When I turned around to face my wife I remember she was short and petite and her thick black hair was parted in the middle. Her bronze face was rather long and narrow at the chin. Since I was wearing a wool checkered coat, and she was wrapped in some sort of blanket garment, the weather must have been quite cool in that region. I am wondering now if the proprietor would have let her in the saloon, even though she wasn't drinking anything. I'm sure discrimination was rampant in those days, and since she was not only a woman but an Indian as well, I'm wondering how she would have been normally treated in a saloon in those days. Since I don't recall the saloon being crowded and I didn't stay long, maybe no one cared to make an issue of it. Of course, maybe the size of my rifle had something to do with it.

I can recall pushing open those swinging doors and walking out into the bright sunshine and onto the street. The street seemed to be a yellow color, as if it were mostly sand. On my left, I remember some kind of wooden building that may have been a feed mill. My pretty little Paiute wife never said a word all through the dream, but just continued to follow along about 5 feet behind me. Actually, I never spoke a word to her either.

It was a problem trying to find some information on the Paiute tribe at first, because I hadn't the slightest idea how to spell it. It is also somewhat of a coincidence that this tribe is found in Utah, the same state as my pen pal.

The fact that I never heard of this tribe before this dream seems to only add more evidence of this being another experience from a past life. It's interesting to note the contrast of my physical body from the Confederate soldier to the man with the hunting rifle. They are just about opposite, and neither one would describe me today.

CHAPTER XVII

THE BLACK COACH

Since I had filled out the form the National Archives sent to me and mailed it back to them, I was waiting for their reply. Hopefully, the personal information I requested about General Samuel McGowan would be available at the Archives, and hopefully it would coincide with the details of my dream. I couldn't wait to read about his physical description. There were no photographs in color during his lifetime, and the only way I could confirm the vision of him in my dream was to read his military records. Of course I was also hoping there would be some detailed explanation of his wounds suffered in numerous battles. I had to know about that left leg injury. It was so important to me it was becoming an obsession. These searches for military records are probably very time consuming, and with the recent interest in Civil War history, they are probably quite busy with similar requests.

During this waiting period, another brief but colorful dream came to me. I was sitting in my yard reading the newspaper when I began to experience a heaviness in my eyelids. As hard as I tried I couldn't keep my eyes open. I suddenly found myself a passenger in a horse drawn coach, riding through the woods on a dirt road. I felt a bump and as I looked out the window of the coach

I saw that the right rear wheel was coming off.

Apparently the driver was aware of the problem and brought the horse to a stop, just as the wheel came loose and began rolling. It rolled several yards onto the grass before it fell flat. I opened the door of the coach and stepped down just as the coachman was climbing down from the driver's seat. He walked over to the fallen wheel and lifted it to its rim. I watched as he rolled the large spoked wheel over to the axle. It was then that I noticed the axle was split and damaged. He seemed to be telling me exactly how he intended to repair the axle but I don't recall what he was saying. Assuming it would take awhile for the coachman to re-attach the wheel, I walked over to the edge of the woods to look for a fairly comfortable place to sit. A big tree nearby looked inviting, but as I approached it I could see that the base of the tree was a fused mass of white lumpy roots. I looked around for a better place to sit and finally decided to sit on the grass. As I watched the coachman working on the problem of trying to mount the wheel back on the axle I awoke.

This dream had nothing to do with the Civil War, but it appeared to take place in eighteenth century Europe. The coach was black with gold trim, and a fancy gold pattern or design was painted across the door of the coach. The wheels on the coach were painted a light green, as I recall the seats in the coach were also a light green.

The coachman was a tall thin young man in his mid 20's perhaps. He had light brown hair and wore a long black coat. He seemed quite cheerful in spite of our mishap, as he talked constantly while working on the axle. There didn't seem to be any other passengers in the coach and I don't know why I didn't offer to help the coachman re-attach the wheel. Somehow, I just thought it was his job and I shouldn't interfere. I didn't experience any fear or apprehension. I seemed to have confidence in the coachman that we would soon be on our way.

If the dream of the black coach was a brief look at another past life, it seems to fit in a time frame of history that so far I have not experienced. It was a beautiful coach, and the fact that I was the only passenger may indicate it may have been my coach, and the driver may have been in my employ. Perhaps this was one rare time in any of my lives that I was a man of financial means. This dream also indicates to me that the dreams of my past lives are not finished. At this time, I have not had a recurring experience with any of my past life dreams except those of the Civil War, which is why this is the main subject of this book.

This dream came upon me just as the Civil War dreams of the bridge and the battlefield. They all came to me while I was reading the newspaper. It almost seems as if my reading sometimes puts me in a hypnotic trance, which propels me back in time to a past life. I don't encourage these journeys back in time while I'm reading, but they do seem to sneak up on me. I don't know why they occur when they do or why I awake from these dreams when I do. In all three instances of falling asleep while reading and reliving a past life, there has never been anything or anyone to awaken me.

I find it interesting that in several of these past life dreams, I wasn't experiencing a painful or traumatic episode of my life. Many of these dreams were more of a learning experience. For example, my dream of the Confederate soldier standing in the wheatfield in his tan uniform was not upsetting to me in any way. There were no shots being fired or being chased by the Federal troops. In fact, it was a picture of tranquility. However, the same dream repeated itself the following night. It was as if it was important for me to realize and remember the difference in his uniform, than what I was accustomed to in my brief knowledge of Civil War history in this lifetime.

It didn't take me long after the second dream to wonder why the soldier was in a tan uniform, and what was the purpose of the red ornamentation around his belt and on the top of his hat. It's almost like being shown a problem in school and the teacher instructs the class to solve the problem. You are not given any clues, you just have to do your research. It's also interesting to me that I don't find anything strange or unusual happening to me or around me during these past life dreams. Everything seems normal, and in spite of the traumatic moments of battle, the circumstances seem understandable and acceptable. It is when I awake back here in the twentieth century that I am full of questions about what just took place and why.

When these dreams occur, it seems that I not only take on a whole different appearance, but even my thoughts and actions are consistent with that part of my past life. For example, when I was reliving my life in my dreams of the Civil War, my thoughts were mainly of survival. Victory almost always seemed to be out of reach, considering there were only about 12 of us against impossible odds in many of my dreams. In my dream of General McGowan, I felt a caring respect and thought of him as a "father" figure. When I awoke, I didn't have the slightest idea who he was until I saw his photo in that bookstore at the mall. Also, I found out from that brief information in that book that I was about 10 years older than he in this lifetime, compared to his age during the Civil War. In this lifetime I certainly wouldn't think of a man who is 10 years my junior as a "father" figure. In these dreams of the Civil War I suddenly became a very tall thin young man of about 23 years of age struggling to survive. I felt no hatred for the Federal troops, nor did I have any political thoughts on the war. I was just a young man trying to do my duty and trying to stay alive.

As for the young medieval soldier on that big white

horse, I was surprised and afraid when the townspeople turned on us, but I didn't want to show my fear. There were plenty of us to fight off any attack, as there seemed to be no end to that long procession. I felt protected and secure for that reason, but I still was feeling very uneasy and couldn't wait to leave that town behind us.

As for the hunter in the bar, my thoughts were few. I just wanted a drink to wash down the dust in my throat and to be left alone. I realized my wife was behind me waiting for me, and I remember thinking of her as my Paiute squaw. As I mentioned earlier, I had never heard of this tribe before, and when I awoke and did some research, I was surprised to find this tribe does indeed exist.

My thoughts during my arrest as a merchant in ancient Greece was of surprise and apprehension. When the magistrate informed me I would be incarcerated for not paying my taxes, I felt defiant and hostile. I felt that if my plan of forcing the guards to kill me succeeded, I would be the victorious one. Of course, I don't know if my plan was successful. It seems that becoming awake at these crucial moments always liberates me.

Perhaps I will one day return to one of these past lives, or perhaps it is meant for me to experience even more past lives in these vivid and memorable dreams. I do not think I have experienced the last of them.

CHAPTER XVIII

THE ARCHIVES

As the weeks went by I waited patiently for another letter from the National Archives in Washington, D. C. At the time I sent the request for information on General McGowan's military record, I had not authorized the use of my credit card for the copy fee, as I wanted to be sure that information was available on file. After six weeks from the time I sent in my original request form, I was notified the military records were on file and copies would be sent to me after I send the necessary fee.

My original request form was accompanied by a note specifically requesting any documents they may have on file of his medical records. I also mentioned I was interested in any documents that would describe General McGowan's physical appearance. They informed me that they had made copies of his entire file, so the very next day I sent the research fee to the National Archives Trust fund in Atlanta, Georgia. I don't know why the fee had to be sent to Atlanta rather than Washington, D.C. but I assume they have their reasons.

After waiting another two weeks to receive my copies of General McGowan's file, I must admit my patience w as running thin. I began to regret that I chose not to pay for the research fee with my credit card, as this was an option that would have saved me a lot of time. However, when I finally received the copies of the documents I requested, I was surprised to find 35 copies of various military documents. Many of them were notes written by Army physicians. Since he was wounded so often throughout the war, these notes are verifications of General McGowan's inability to return to active duty until a specified future date. Even though there was a note enclosed explaining that due to the age of these documents they may not be as clear as I would like, my biggest challenge was in trying to decipher the army physician's handwriting.

After carefully reading the copies of the medical notes written by the army physicians who attended to him, I am at last able to confirm that General McGowan was indeed shot and wounded in his left leg below the knee on May 2, 1863 at the battle of Chancellorsville. Another medical note also confirms he was wounded in the left foot on May 3, 1863. The notes do not state if he suffered a gun shot wound in the foot or if it was injured in another way. Perhaps the foot was injured when the leg was shot. One of the army physician's notes states, "I have been in attendance upon General Samuel McGowan who is suffering from a gun shot wound of the left leg, near severed the limb. The whole limb has been weakened. This round drilled in the shin bone."

At long last I was able to confirm his wounded left leg as he stood wobbling before me on the field that day. In both medical notes recommending an extension of leave of absence from active duty, they are dated many months from the time of his injuries. Perhaps his left foot healed faster than his left leg because his physician recommended another 60 days extension of his leave of absence on a note dated August 10, 1863. In the note dealing with his injured left leg, he was given a 30 day extension of leave on a note dated Dec. 7, 1863. Apparently, even after 7 months convalescing he still needed at least another 30 days before resuming active duty.

In all the reference books I've looked in at the library and at the bookstores these many months since that dream, I haven't seen any mention of the nature of his wounds, only that he was wounded four times. I am so glad the National Archives had General McGowan's medical records on file. It at last reinforces my dream of him as having an injured left leg below the knee.

I mentioned a quote in one of the chapters of Dr. Holzer's book, *Great American Ghost Stories*, in reference to General McGowan's returning to active duty but still not able to walk well. This quote made no mention of the nature of his wounds that consequently made walking difficult for him. He could have been wounded in his right leg or could even have suffered a back injury, either of which would make walking difficult. He was injured during the battle of Chancellorsville in the month of May in 1863. The weather in my dream of him on the battlefield that day was sunny and pleasant, as would be typical of the month of May. In my dream, I just assumed he fell off his horse and was trying to get up, but his left leg was caving in on him. If he was shot in the left leg or his foot at that particular time, I didn't see any blood, but yet I knew he had a lower left leg injury that he never really recovered from, it would explain the absence of blood and his difficulty in still maintaining his balance.

I have not heard or read anywhere of a defeat on the battlefield that would have resulted in his surrender, but as I mentioned before, the tide of battle can turn very quickly. If his capture was only momentary, it probably would have not been mentioned in the records. I'm sure many incidents have happened on a battlefield that never made the history books. I'm assuming my request to the National Archives for copies of any documents that may describe General McGowan's physical appearance were not available. In my dream he had reddish brown hair that was streaked with gray. He also had what appeared to be pale blue eyes. I would have liked to have gotten a verification on those physical details. I thought a physical description would be standard information in a soldier's military record, but perhaps these documents were lost over the years.

Among the other documents I received from the National Archives were several hand written letters by Field and Company officers addressed to the Secretary of War recommending the promotion of Colonel Samuel McGowan to Brig. General. The following are two examples of those hand written requests. Although the first one was very difficult to understand initially, a lot of hard concentration paid off. When I finally deciphered the signature on these notes, I realized they were written by the C. S. Sect. Of Treasury, C. G. Memminger. Either he must have had arthritis or was writing these notes while riding horseback.

The petition is signed with the signatures of 57 officers. Although the petition was written with very clear and beautiful handwriting, many of the signatures are difficult to understand. Most of these documents are copies of medical certificates, describing General McGowan's promotions and even his parole as a prisoner of war after General Robert E. Lee's surrender. You will need a lot of concentration and perhaps a magnifying glass to read the surgeon's report on Gen. McGowan's leg wound, but it is there.

Hon C. G. Memminger
Richmond Va
Dec 24/62

Enclosing petition
for the appt of Col.
S. McGowan Brig Genl
2 papers

Recd. Dec 29/62

Richmond
Dec 24. 1862

Dear Sir

I wrote you yesterday strongly recommending Col: McGowan to the place vacated by the death of the lamented Gregg. I have the pleasure now of adding the enclosed petition to which I would be glad to add any force which my recommendation can give.

Very truly Yrs
C G Memminger

Hon: J. A. Seddon,
Secty of War

This letter and the two that follow were written by C. S. Sect. Of Treasury, G. M. Memminger. They were addressed to the C. S. Sect. Of War, strongly endorsing the promotion of Colonel Samuel McGowan to the title of Brigadier General.

Richmond
Jan 10. 1863

My Dear Mr Secty
I feel so much interest in Colonel McGowan's being appointed to succeed Gregg, that I venture to trespass on you to be assured whether his papers are before you. He has the recommendation of both Genl Hill — and has that of Gregg himself for promotion. I most cordially endorse all that has been said in his favor and wish that he may succeed to the place.

Very truly Yrs
C G Memminger.

Hon:
J. A. Seddon
Secty War,

Hon. C. G. Memminger
Richd, Va.
Jan. 10/63 72. W.D.

In reference to the promotion of Col. McGowan to succeed Genl. Gregg.

Brig Genl—

File

Recd Jan 10/63

Appl. M. 19 file

Hon C. G. Memminger
Richmond Va
Dec 23/62

Recommending Col McGowan for Brig. Genl. in place of the late Genl Gregg—

Respy Referred to the President
JAS Secy

Secty of War
let Col. McGowan be appointed
J.D.

To A.G.
Appointed JAS Secy

Recd Dec 23/62
Recorded Jan 22/63

Richmond
Dec 23. 1862

Hon: Jas. A. Seddon,
Secty of War.

Sir

Col: McGowan's friends propose to present him as a fit officer to take the place of the late Genl Gregg. I beg very respectfully to join in the presentment, and to ask that he may be considered as I regard him one of the most estimable men, and good officers in our South Carolina Regiments. He has long occupied a prominent position in our State and is highly esteemed by all who know him. He has been twice wounded in Battle and has been actively engaged in the battles at Richmond and Fredericksburg.

Very truly yrs
C. G. Memminger,

Bivouac near Port Royal Va
Decr 18th 1862

To the Hon: Secretary of War

We the undersigned Field and Company officers of the 1st Regiment of Rifles, 12th Infantry, and 14th Infantry South Carolina Volunteers of the Brigade lately commanded by the lamented Brig Genl Maxcy Gregg of Genl A P Hills light division would respectfully request that Colonel Samuel McGowan of the 14th Regiment South Carolina Volunteers may be appointed to fill the vacancy occasioned by the death of Brig Genl Gregg. In our opinion Col McGowan is an officer whose education, gallantry, firmness and experience eminently fit him for the position of Brigadier General. He served in the war with Mexico as a Captain and has been in the service of the Confederate States ever since the present war commenced and has shown constant and untiring devotion to duty in every capacity in which he was placed.

A Perrin Capt Co D 14th S.C.V. actg Lt Col
Joseph N Brown Capt Co E 14th Regt S C Vols
H P Griffith 1st Lt Co "E" 14th Regt S.C.V.
S. L. Dorroh 2 Lt " " " "
N. Austin 2d Do " " " "
Jas M McCarley Capt Co H " " "
J. H Williams 2d Lt
G W Jones 2 Lieut Co C
J M Miller Lt comdg C
Edw Croft Capt Company "K" 14th Regt S C V
J C Steedman Lieut " " " "
John M. Bell " " B " "
W J Stevens " " K " "
J K Allen " " K " "

A. B. Hines 1st Lt Co (A) 14th Regt
Sidney Carter – 2nd Lt co A
H. F. Crooker Sergt com. comp B
Jno. G. Barkley Lt of Co commanding Co 14th

G. McD Miller Capt. Co. G. Orrs Regt Rifles
J. L. Charles Jr 2nd Lt Co G Orrs Rifles
H. Rogers 2 Liet Co H
A. K. Sullivan 1st Lieut Co C Orrs Regt of Rifles
Geo. M. Bigby
J. H. Gentry 2nd Lt Co F Orrs Regt Rifles
P. Jennery 3 Lt
Jno. G. Edwards Capt & A.C.S.
J. Wardlaw Perrin Capt & A.Q.M. Orrs Regt Rifles

Capt co B 12th Regt S.C.V.
R. L. Simmons 3rd Lieut
J. C. Neely Capt Co K
H. P. Shade 1st Lieut Co. K
John M. Hooker 2 Lieut

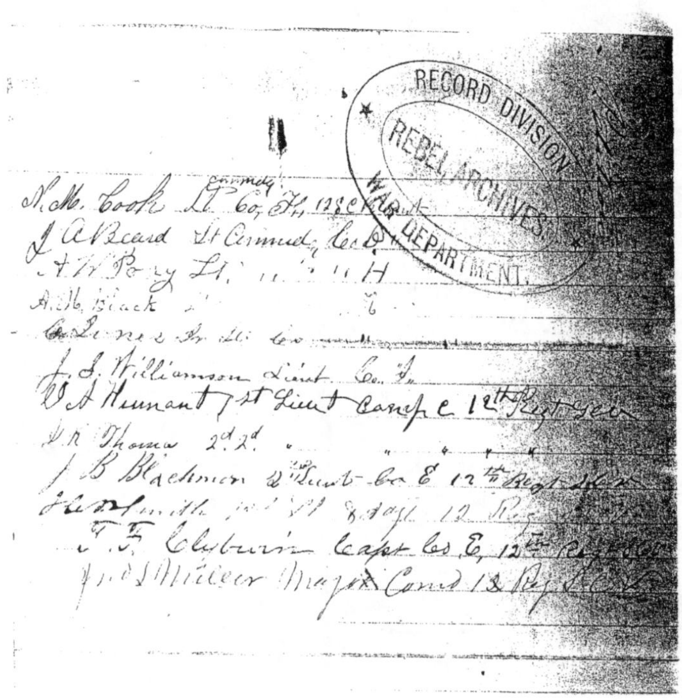
RECORD DIVISION
REBEL ARCHIVES
WAR DEPARTMENT

N. M. Cook Lt Co. F [illegible]
J. A. Beard [illegible]
J. S. Williamson Lieut. Co. F
[illegible] 1st Lieut Comp C 12th Regt [illegible]
J. B. Blackmon 2nd Lieut Co E 12th Regt [illegible]
T. F. Clyburn Capt Co E 12th Regt [illegible]
[illegible] Miller Major Comd 12 Reg [illegible]

This well-written letter of petition on the preceding pages was addressed to the Sect. Of War and signed by 57 officers. Although most of the signatures are illegible due to time and the poor quality of the copies, I decided to include them anyway. Perhaps someone will detect a familiar name.

(CONFEDERATE.) 6

Mc staff

Samuel McGowan
Brig Genl McGowans Brig

Appears on an

Inspection Report

of McGowan's Brigade of South Carolina Volunteers, commanded by Brig. Gen. Samuel McGowan.

Report dated Near Petersburg Va Dec 27, 1864

Date of muster of organization into service ...., 186 .

Term of service ....

Absent commissioned officers accounted for:

By what authority Leave of indulgence Genl Lee

Date Dec 1, 1864

Remarks: ....

Inspection Report P, No. 46; inclosure 8.

(654) A S Douglas Copyist.

4120

(CONFEDERATE.)

Mc 14 S.C.

Saml. McGowan
Col P.A.C.S.

Appears on a

Register

of Appointments, Confederate States Army.

State S.C.

To whom report 14 S.C. Regt.

Date of appointment May 10, 1862.

Date of confirmation Oct 7, 1862.

To take rank Apr. 11, 1862.

Date of acceptance ...., 186 .

Delivered Genl. J. R. Anderson

Secretary of War G. W. R.

Remarks: Promoted Brig. Genl. Jan. 17, 1863.

Confed. Arch., Chap. 1, File No. 86, page 17

(635) Geo S. Preston Copyist.

5797

The register on the right is significant, for it proclaims the promotion of Colonel McGowan to Brigadier General.

McGowan Samuel
General

Appointed assistant to the
Q. M. General - P.C.

See G.O. 11. April 10. 1861 - Beauregard.
Dept S.C. Ga & Fla

McGowan, Samuel

Brig. Gen.

P.A.C.S.

Subject: Leave

Special Order Number 180/21

Aug 1, 1864

Adjutant & Inspector General's Office, Confederate States, contains information relative to the man named, on the subject mentioned above.

(CONFEDERATE.)

Mc

Saml McGowan
Brig. General

Appears on a

Register

of Appointments, Confederate States Army.

State S.C.
To whom report Genl. R. E. Lee
Date of appointment Apr. 23, 1863.
Date of confirmation Apr. 23, 1863.
To take rank Jan. 17, 1863.
Date of acceptance June 9, 1863.
Delivered Genl R. E. Lee
Secretary of War J. A. S.
Remarks:

Confed. Arch., Chap. 1, File No. 86, page 10

(635) Geo S Preston Copyist.

5707

×McGowan S.

Brig Genl. Comdg 2 Brig Hills Light Div

See personal papers of

Oliver E. Edwards

, Co. ......, 13 Reg't SC

INDEX CARD OF CONFEDERATE RECORDS.

(539) This card must not be taken from the files.

Write nothing above this line.

McGowan S.

Brig Genl

Feby 5. 1864

Having reported for duty, will assume command of his Brigade relieving Brig Gen A Perrin its present Commander, x x

S.O. 34 ANV - Loc - 1864

(A. G. O. 124—1.) c 3—684

Write nothing above this line.

Samuel McGowan

Colonel

Jan 19, 1863 - Announced as Brig General to report to Lt Gen Jackson for assignment to command of Gregg's Brigade, A.P. Hills Div. 2 Corps ANV.

2-88-40

(A. G. O. 124—1.) c 3—684

Surgeon Michels' certificate
Richmond May 10th 1863. –
Gen. S. McGowan, having applied for a certificate upon which to ground an application for a leave of absence, I certify that I have carefully examined him, and find him suffering from a severe gun shot wound of the left leg. I further declare my belief that he will not be fit for duty in a less period than sixty days (60). –
Middleton Michel Surg.

endorsed
May 10th 1863
Approved & Respectfully forwarded
By order Medl Director R. S. J. Peebles
Surgeon P.A.C.S.

Approved
By order of Gen Winder
W. S. Winder
A. A. G.

Abbeville S. C.
30 June 1863
I certify that for several weeks past I have been in attendance upon Gen. Saml McGowan, who is suffering from a gun shot wound of the left leg near the ankle joint. The whole limb has been much swollen, the wound filled with unhealthy granulations [illegible]

These hand written messages deal with the crucial evidence I had been searching for concerning Gen. McGowan's gunshot wound of his left leg below the knee. Unfortunately, the terrible penmanship of physicians has been an object of humor for years, and I guess those who served in the Civil War were no exception. The severity of this wound is described in the last message dated June 30, 1863.

Brig^r Genl. Saml. McGowan of Comd of late Ge
Penders Division having applied for a certificate on which to ground an application
for leave of Absence. I do hereby certify that
~~I have carefully~~ examined this Officer
and find that he is still suffering from
a wound in the left foot received
at the Battle of Chancellorsville on the 3^d May 1863
And that in consequence thereof he is in
my opinion unfit for duty. I further
declare my belief that he will not be
able to resume his duties in a less
period than sixty days–

Columbia S. C.
August 10th 1863

J. Ford Prioleau Surg PA
and Surg. Post

Board of Examiners for Furloughs and Discharges.

GENERAL HOSPITALS, COLUMBIA, S. C.

Brig. Gen. S. McGowan of the C. S. Army

~~Regiment of~~ ~~Company~~ having applied for a certificate on which to ground an application for leave of absence, the Board hereby certify that it has carefully examined this officer and find that he is convalescing from Gun Shot wound of left leg recd. 2nd May 1863 wound not healed

And that in consequence thereof, he is, in the opinion of the Board, unfit for duty. It further declares its belief that he will not be able to resume his duties in a less period than Thirty days. Extension

A W Thomson
Senior Surgeon of Board.

POST OFFICE: Abbeville C.H. S.C.
COUNTY: Abbeville Dist
DATE: December 7th 1863

This notice from General Hospitals dated Dec. 7th, 1863 indicates Gen. McGowan still had not recovered from the left leg wound received on May 2, 1863.

Head-Quarters,

MEDICAL DEPARTMENT, FOURTH CONGRESSIONAL DISTRICT,

Edgefield C. H. SC Jan 14 1864

We certify that we have carefully examined ~~Private~~ Brig Genl. S McGowan Wilcox's ~~Company~~ Division ~~Regiment~~, and find him, in our opinion, unable to perform the duties of ~~a Soldier~~ an Officer because of Gun shot wound in leg

And we further declare it our belief that the said ~~Soldier~~ Officer will not be able to resume his duties in a period less than {30} thirty days; and as he is not accessible to a Hospital Board, and is unable to travel without aggravating his present physical condition, we would respectfully recommend that his furlough be extended for that period of time under General Order No. 141, A. & I. G. O.

J. P. Cameron
Asst. Surgeon, P. A. C. S.
President Ex. Board.
McTaggart

Examining Board of Conscripts.

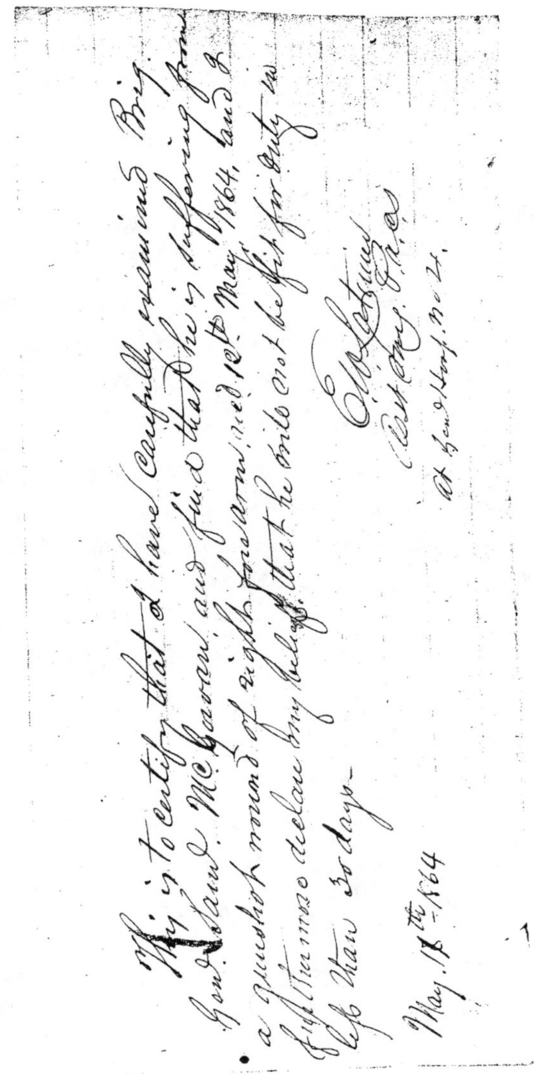

This is to certify that I have carefully examined Brig. Gen. Saml. McGowan and find that he is suffering from a gunshot wound of right forearm, received 12th May, 1864, and I further declare my belief that he will not be fit for duty in less than 30 days.

May 18th 1864

[illegible]
Asst. Surg. P.A.C.S.
At Genl Hosp. No 1.

General McGowan's misfortune continued with a gunshot wound of his right forearm, received at the battle of Spottsylvania, C. H.

Certificate Recommending Extension of Furlough.

Brig Genl McGowan of Co. ——— Reg't, McGowan's Brigade, (Post Office Abbeville C.H. S.C.) having been granted a Furlough on the 17th day of May 1864, at Richmond Va by Ord of Secty of War, on Surg Certificate and having appeared before this Board for recommendation for *extension* of Furlough, we do hereby certify that we have carefully examined him and find that (make a full statement of the case.) he has a severe gunshot wound of forearm, received at battle of Spottsylvania C.H. May 12th 1864

And in consequence thereof, he will not, in our opinion, be fit for duty in a less period than (30) days, for which time we recommend an extension of his Furlough.

H. F. Andrews *Surgeon P. A. C. S.*
C. N. Coleman [illegible]
A. D. Hoke [illegible]
BOARD.

Place.} Examining Board Abbeville S.C.

Date.} June 18th 1864

[DUPLICATE.]

(CONFEDERATE.)

Mc

S. McGowan

Brig. Genl. S.C.

Appears on a Register of

General Hospital No. 4,
Richmond, Virginia.

Date May 11, 1863

Brigade

Remarks: May 11, 63. Transfd to Wilmington

Confed. Arch., Chap. 6, File No. 178, page 8

O. T. Taylor
(635) 155 Copyist.

(CONFEDERATE.)

Mc

S. McGowan

Brig. General

Appears on a Register of

General Hospital No. 4,
Richmond, Virginia.

Disease V. S. R. Leg

Admitted May 15, 1864.

Returned to duty, 186 .

Deserted, 186 .

Discharged from service, 186 .

Sent to General Hospital, 186 .

Furloughed June 1, 1864.

Died, 186 .

Remarks:

Confed. Arch., Chap. 6, File No. 178, page 136

O. T. Taylor
(635) 163 Copyist.

These are two more samples of General McGowan's medical records. Apparently he had a problem with his right leg on May 15, 1864.

(CONFEDERATE.)

Mc | S.C.

S. McGowan
Brig. Genl South Carolina

Appears on an

Inspection Report

of Maj. Gen. C. M. Wilcox's Division, Lt. Gen. A. P. Hill's Corps, Army of Northern Virginia, commanded by Brig. Gen. J. H. Lane.

Report dated Near Petersburg, Va
Feby 28, 1865

Date of muster of organization into service. 1861.

Term of service War

Absent commissioned officers accounted for:

By what authority

Date , 186 .

Remarks:

Inspection Report P, No. 64; inclosure 11.

(654) O. T. Taylor Copyist.

4251

(CONFEDERATE.)

Mc

S. McGowan
Brig Genl S.C. Troops

Appears on an

Inspection Report

of Maj. Gen. C. M. Wilcox's Division, Lt. Gen. A. P. Hill's Corps.

Report dated Near Petersburg Va
Jan 30, 1865.

Date of muster of organization into service. 1861.

Term of service For the war

Absent commissioned officers accounted for:

By what authority

Date , 186 .

Remarks:

Inspection Report P, No. 53; inclosure 1.

(654) J. B. Hyatt Copyist.

4194

(Confederate.)

Mc

S. McGowan
Brig Genl P. A. C. S.

Name appears as a signature to a

Parole of Prisoners of War,

belonging to the Army of Northern Virginia, this day surrendered by General Robert E. Lee, C. S. A., commanding said Army, to Lieut. Genl. U. S. Grant, commanding Armies of United States.

Done at Appomattox Court House, Virginia, April 9, 1865.

Number of roll: 224

J. Henderson
Copyist.

(CONFEDERATE.)

Mc

S. McGowan
Brig. Gen S. C. Troops

Appears on an

Inspection Report

of Wilcox's Light Division, Lt. Gen. A. P. Hill's Corps, commanded by Maj. Gen. C. M. Wilcox.

Report dated Near Petersburg Va Sept 30, 1864.

Date of muster of organization into service ...., 186/.

Term of service For the war

Absent commissioned officers accounted for:

By what authority

Date ...., 186 .

Remarks:

Inspection Report P, No. 24; inclosure 6.

(654) H. G. Taylor
Copyist.

3866

The memo on the left is very significant. General McGowan appeared as a paroled prisoner of war after the surrender of General Robert E. Lee.

General McGowan was again wounded on May 12, 1864 with a severe gunshot wound of his right forearm, received at the battle of Spottsylvania, as several physician's notes indicated. One of the notes was dated June 15, 1864 and recommends an extended furlough of 30 days to recuperate from this wound. It must have been very difficult for General McGowan to report back to active duty after a long convalescence of a serious wound only to suffer another wound during another battle. He must have been a very decorated and honored war hero. To consider the possibility of my having served with him in that past lifetime is a provocative thought indeed.

Now that my wait was over to receive the copies of General McGowan's military record from the archives, and I have confirmed that crucial bit of evidence about his left leg wound, I was wondering if Kristin, my pen pal from Salt Lake City, would find any information on Sgt. Albert Richardson. She had mentioned to me in our correspondence of a large Genealogical Library located in Salt Lake City where many people from all over the country go to trace their ancestor's military history. She told me she would go there in the near future and see if there may possibly be a Sgt. Albert Richardson listed. Since this was the name that passed through my mind during the hypnosis session with Dr. Holzer, I had no way of confirming this to have been my name in that past lifetime. However, it was worth a try to see if they had any information.

About a week after I received my information from the Archives, I received a large envelope from Krisitn. In her letter, she told me she was unable to locate anything on Albert Richardson at the Genealogical Library, but provided me with 60 pages of information she accessed from the internet on her computer, most of which were available sources of information to further research material on the Civil War. Although this information is available on Civil War history, my main objective these past few years was to try to verify as much as possible the historical details of all my dreams of the Civil War. To become a scholar of Civil War history is not my goal. My only interest was to confirm to a reasonable degree that my observations and memories during these dreams were historically accurate, such as the uniforms and weapons, which proved to be authenticated by my research.

As for Sgt. Albert Richardson, I still don't have any information as to whether this name that appeared to me during the hypnosis session was actually my name as the Confederate soldier, or perhaps as I mentioned before, it may have been the name of the famous Civil War correspondent whose name, for reasons unknown, crossed my mind at that time. Since I'm sure I didn't reach the military fame that General McGowan did, perhaps I was born into obscurity and died the same way. However, I'm certain I was that tall Confederate soldier, whether he had a name or not.

CHAPTER XIX

THE DIGGING DETAIL

As the weeks went by my thoughts were of finalizing my past lives dream project. I had catalogued my dreams in the chronological order in which they occurred, and the time I had spent on historical research and typing began to come to a close. I assumed that by now my dreams would take on the more normal pattern of the usual mundane reflections of my life in the present. However, I was surprised to experience two more dreams of the Civil War, both occurring in the same week, and just about three months after the dream of the black coach. As with the other dreams about the Civil War I couldn't get them out of my mind.

The first dream occurred early in the week one afternoon in late June while I was sitting in my yard composing a letter to my pen pal, Kristin. I had completed one full page of my letter when I suddenly became very sleepy. As soon as I closed my eyes, I found myself watching a work detail of three Confederate soldiers digging a hole in the side of a steep dirt hill. From the area where I was standing, I appeared to be about 25 feet from the three men. The hill was approximately 40 feet high and the top of it was covered with thick green foliage of bushes, grass and trees. Although my attention was focused on these three men digging into the side of the hill, I knew I was in a valley surrounded by trees. On my right I could see a wide inclined dirt road that seemed to lead up to the other side of the hill. There were several Confederate soldiers walking up and down that steep dirt road, but I paid very little attention to them. This was no little foot path winding through the forest, it was wide enough to accommodate two teams of horses pulling a wagon to pass each other. I was also aware of other soldiers milling about, as everyone seemed busy doing their chores on this sunny hot day.

As I stood there watching, one of the three men was digging in the ground several feet from the hill, while the other two worked at digging a large hole in the side of the hill. The dirt was a light brown and seemed almost like dry powder. Although the men were working hard and perspiring profusely, at least the dirt was giving way to the shovels, a task that would be made more difficult indeed if the hill were made of clay and rock.

One of the men suddenly stepped back several feet and rested on his shovel. He then reached into his back pocket and pulled out a red and white handkerchief. As he proceeded to wipe his face and neck, I could see that his gray jacket had a big wet spot between his shoulder blades. He appeared to be the oldest of the three, possibly about 30 years of age, while the other two seemed to be in their early 20's. He looked a little aggravated as he walked over to the other soldier who was also digging that large hole in the hillside. As he stood there trying to talk to the man who shared his work detail, he was ignored. The other man seemed to be too anxious to get that hole dug to stop and talk, as he hacked away at that dirt with energetic ferocity. Since he was being ignored by his digging partner, he walked over to the other young man who seemed to be less enthusiastic about his digging detail. As he approached him, the young man looked toward the soldier who appeared to have a gripe and stopped digging and leaned on his shovel to listen.

The hole dug into the side of the hill so far was quite large, about 4 feet in diameter and about 2 feet deep. The whole scene was in such vivid color, from the smooth brown hillside to the various shades of green of the shrubs and forest on top of the hill, as well as the trees that surrounded us. I don't know why my attention was riveted to those three men, as they didn't seem to be aware of my presence. Perhaps they were digging as part of a punishment detail, and I was assigned to keep an eye on them, or maybe they were digging a cave and a ditch for some reason. I doubt that these men were digging as part of a punishment detail due to the enthusiastic energy put into this job, especially by the man who would not stop digging for a minute to listen to his partner.

As the men continued to dig this whole scene before me began to slowly fade as I was starting to awake from this dream. Suddenly I heard a loud voice behind me say what sounded like, "Claysboro, Tennessee." When I was fully awake, I found my unfinished letter to Kristin on my lap and immediately explained to her in the letter about the dream. I also mentioned that this was the first time in my dreams of the Civil War that I heard the name of a place. I wondered if there really was a Claysboro, Tennessee and if it was located in such rugged looking country as in my dream.

I received a reply to my letter from Kristin about two weeks later. She told me she had done some research on her computer but could find no listing of Claysboro, however, she found a Clay County located in Northern Middle Tennessee near the Kentucky border. She also discovered there is a town called Gainsboro, which she said sounds very much like Claysboro. In my next letter to her I thanked her for her research and decided to write to the Chamber of Commerce in Nashville. I told them I would appreciate any information they can send to me about Tennessee and its history, and that I was particularly interested in any photos and information around the Gainsboro area if that information is available.

About a week later I received a colorful and informative vacation guide book from the Tennessee Tourist Development in Nashville. The book was arranged in three divisions, West, Middle and East. Each section contained detailed information on all the attractions, historic sites, state parks, etc. The guidebook also contained a map of the state, which I immediately began to examine in search of a place called Claysboro. The only town I could find on the map that came close to it was Gainsboro, as Kristin informed me earlier. Suddenly I began to think about Clay County. Could it have been known as Clay Borough 140 years ago?

While browsing through the guidebook, I was hoping to see a photo of a rough terrain of hills and forests. When I came to the section in the book dealing with the Middle area of Tennessee, the first page proclaimed its historical significance. As I searched further through the guidebook it mentioned its Civil War history, which included the city of Gainsboro. It was listed as having strong pioneer and Civil War heritage. Although the book was permeated with beautiful color photos of the various attractions, state parks and campsites, I could not find a photo that came close to the scenery in my dream. Of course, this dream took place in only a small area of wilderness, but I had hoped I might see a photo of a similar terrain. I knew my next place of search would be the library.

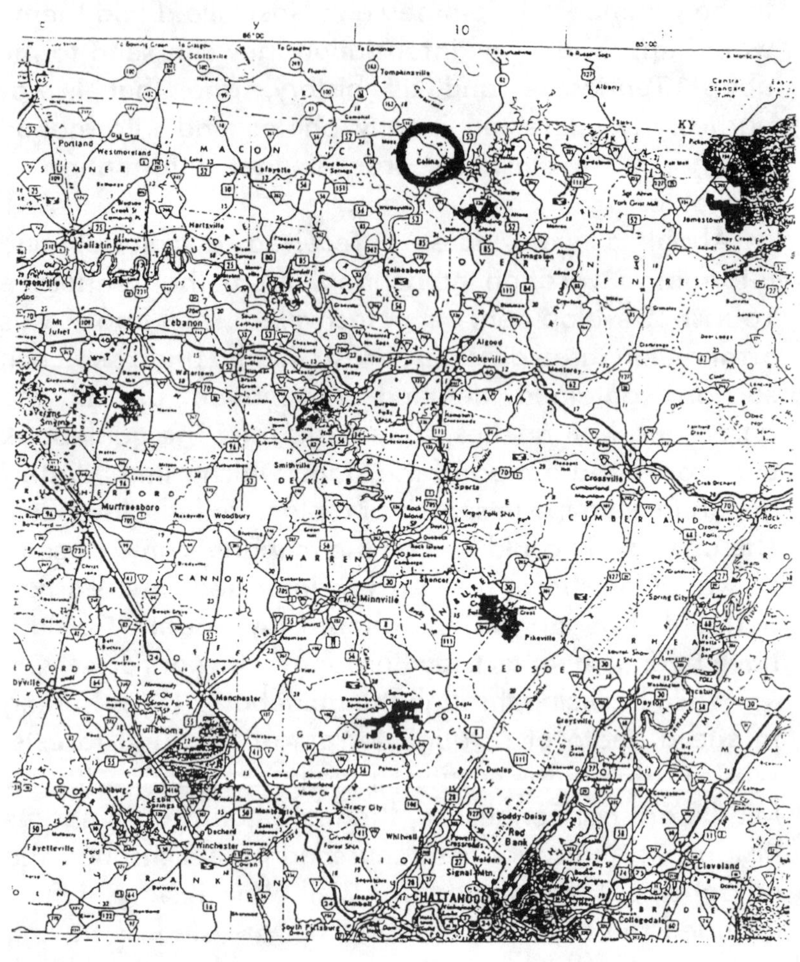

The area I have indicated on the map shows where I may have been in my dream. The town of Celina is located only a few miles from the rugged border of Kentucky in Clay County. Could this area have been known as Clay Borough during the Civil War?

As I entered the library a few days later armed with pad and pen to record whatever I could find on North Central Tennessee, I was surprised to find only one book on the shelf about Tennessee. It was called, *The Tennessee Sampler* by Peter Jenkins and Friends, but as I browsed through the book, it seemed to cover everything you'd ever want to know about Tennessee. It gave a description of Standing Stone State Rustic Park and Forest as being noted for its outstanding scenery, Spring wildflowers, beautiful hardwood forest, Fall colors and other natural diversity. The State Park is situated on 11,000 acres in Overton County, within a triangle formed by highways connecting Livingston, Gainsboro and a town in Clay County called Celina.

Although I found the book to be interesting and informative, I still could not find a photo of this area to satisfy my curiosity. My last thought was to try to find a video travelogue on Tennessee. If there were one available, it would probably cover the entire state, and I just might spot a familiar terrain. This dream had been on my mind every day and I felt driven to discover if there were indeed a Confederate camp set up in that area of Tennessee, and if there were any significance to that digging project.

Several days later I was browsing through a video store at the local mall is search of a travelogue video that may possibly illustrate the area of Kentucky and Tennessee. Although they had no videos on this specific area, I happened to see a video entitled, *Across America*. The information on the video cover briefly described its contents and explained that the film was photographed from a helicopter and gave a close aerial view of the United States including Alaska and Hawaii. I bought the video and had high hopes of finally being able to see the Kentucky/Tennessee border area.

The following day I turned on the TV, pushed the

video into the VCR and waited to see if my curiosity would finally be satisfied. I held the remote in my hand and was prepared to use the stop action button if the helicopter in the film began to hover over that area of rugged terrain. As the movie progressed and beautiful aerial views were shown of New England and New York, I assumed the camera would soon be going South, as this seemed to be the direction it was taking. Soon I was watching areas of the mid-west, and as the camera later began to show the beautiful sights of Texas, I knew the area I wanted to see had been overlooked. Although the video was well worth the time and money, that rugged area had eluded me once again.

My only consolation came about a week later when a conversation with a neighbor seemed to offer some confirmation about the terrain of that area. He had just returned from a vacation tour of the South, and when I asked him if he had traveled through the middle Tennessee/Kentucky border area, he told me he had. When I asked him if this area was a rugged terrain of steep hills and valleys, he confirmed my description was correct.

Since I have not made a personal visit to this area, I can only assume the information he gave me of the description of the terrain reflects the images of my dream. Perhaps I am putting too much emphasis on the name of the place I heard in my dream. It is quite possible that this dream did not even take place in Tennessee, but rather I may have just overheard someone behind me talking about this town in a very loud voice. However, due to the fact that this whole scene of the men digging and the Confederate camp began to slowly fade before my eyes just as that voice boomed loud and clear, I am inclined to think it came from a more divine source.

If the scene in my dream does exist, perhaps it would

not be accessible by auto, and for the moment, a helicopter ride seems out of the question. I know this dream will continue to haunt me until I see for myself whether such a Confederate camp did indeed exist.

CHAPTER XX

THE TRUCE

A few days after the dream of the Confederate digging detail, I had another dream of the Civil War. The circumstances were a little unusual, but it took place in the woods during a skirmish with the Federal troops. It was a dense area of the woods and the plants and foliage were covered with big dark green leaves. The area was so thick with vines and plant life I couldn't even see my own men. All I could see were the legs of a few of them as they lay on their stomachs in the underbrush. It seemed there were more dense bushes and plant life than trees, as I crouched on one knee behind a bush with big green leaves. It seemed more like a jungle than a forest. One would almost expect to hear the roar of a lion or the screech of a monkey.

As I fired my rifle in an area in front of me, the woods was so dense I really couldn't see one Federal trooper. A volley of shots was sporadically returned and I would shoot at the sound and the hint of white smoke that rose from the foliage. I don't know how long we were shooting at each other, but we heard one of the Federal troops call out to us asking for a temporary truce. He said he wanted to meet us in the small clearing that lie between our defense positions. They appeared to have ceased firing momentarily, so I had to make a fast decision. I had only the thick bush I was crouched behind to cover me, and I thought if I stood up to acknowledge their request it may be a trick, and I would be shot. I decided to take the chance but stayed low while I shouted back to them that we agreed to the meeting. Cautiously I stood up and after a brief moment, I began to feel the Federal troops were in earnest.

I motioned to the Confederates near me to go with me. As we began to walk cautiously through the thick underbrush to the clearing, I could see several Federal troopers starting to emerge from their safe haven of dense foliage. They held on to their rifles as we did but they made no threatening gestures. Within a few minutes we reached the clearing and met face to face with the Federal troops. I had four men with me and there were six of them. The speaker of the group looked like an officer. He was a tall distinguished looking man with a mustache, and he appeared to be in his early 30's. His blue uniform was neat and proper, but he and his men looked as if a pile of dirt was dumped on them. The officer stood tall and spoke clearly with an air of authority, despite the fact he was so covered with dirt. I had no idea where they were taking cover to look like this, but he strived to maintain his dignity.

It seemed that their food supply was running low and they assumed we were in the same situation. I admitted that this was indeed the truth. The Federal officer then suggested a 24 hour truce, as both sides needed to replenish our food supply. I turned to look at my men and they all nodded in agreement. I then told the Federal officer we agreed to the 24 hour truce. Even if we did not have much luck finding food, I welcomed the break in the fighting. The other Federal troops who accompanied the officer were watching our negotiation with anticipation, and as soon as we agreed to begin the temporary truce they ran in all directions, presumably to search for food.

As I turned to my men they started to run through the woods in the opposite direction. Left alone, I thought I had better not waste any time. My main concern was where to start looking for food in the middle of a dense woods. I was unfamiliar with the area so I had no idea if there were any farms or fruit trees nearby. The only source of food I could think of was to try to find some blackberry or blueberry bushes. I also was keeping an eye open for rabbits and squirrels. I was making an intense effort to find something to eat, as I knew the shooting would resume in 24 hours. I was still looking for berry bushes when I awoke.

Since I always find myself suddenly thrust into the middle of a situation in all of my dreams of the Civil War, I don't know how long this skirmish was in progress. If we were both admitting to being low on food, perhaps we'd been shooting at each other for several days. Apparently, they were in need of food even more desperately than we if they were the first to call a temporary truce. When I think about this situation, why didn't they just retreat if they thought they couldn't continue the skirmish any longer for lack of food? If they had eased on out of the area we wouldn't have seen them, since the woods were so dense. The only way we would have known something was going on was by the absence of their gunfire. Perhaps they couldn't retreat because they may have had their backs to a steep cliff or some other unsurmountable obstacle. Of course, this may have been just a ploy on the part of the Federal troops to remove themselves from the battle zone without having to surrender or risk further lives. In fact, it's possible it wasn't food they were desperately in need of, but ammunition. While I continued to look for food, I doubt if the Federal troops ever returned to resume our battle.

Several weeks after these two dreams, I was browsing in B. Walton's book store at the mall. I wandered over to the "History" section and noticed a book entitled, *The Life of Johnny Reb* by Bell Irvin Wiley. When I pulled the book from the shelf I opened it to the area near the middle and started to read a page just to get an idea of what the book contained, and to see if it would be of some interest to me. What I read on that page sent a chill up my spine. It was an actual event recorded in the diary of a Confederate soldier whose experience on the battlefield paralleled mine from my dream in my chapter I called "The Carnage." This soldier recorded in his diary that he was hit once in the shoulder and again in the leg but felt no pain, only numbness over his entire body, as was the case with me and the wound in my hip. He also wrote that he lay there in an open field for the rest of the day and into the night without losing consciousness. His thoughts were even as mine in my dream, as he became despondent and feared he would not live to see the dawn, and that he would be buried in a mass grave along with the dead soldiers who lay all around him. He also made mention of the fact his loss of blood had made him cold and he lay there shaking. In my dream, it was only the fact that the sun had set and the evening brought cooler temperatures. I didn't lie there shaking, in fact the cool night air was a blessed relief. Ironically, the soldier who wrote about his experience in his diary was helped by a young Federal who heard his cries for water and aided him throughout the rest of the night. He was later rescued by Confederates who had his wounds tended to and he made a full recovery.

As I put the book back on the shelf I still had goose bumps on my arms and a feeling of shock and surprise, much as how I felt when I first saw General Samuel McGowan's photo in that book of Confederate generals. I couldn't get that book out of my mind for the rest of the evening and I was angry with myself for not buying it when I had it in my hands. The following morning I went straight to that bookstore and hoped it would still be there, as it was the only one on the shelf the day before. As I made my way to the aisle of history books and scanned the shelf, I breathed a sigh of relief. I found the book just where I left it. As soon as I got it home I started to read it from the beginning. I had previously ignored any books of this nature while my dreams of the Civil War were occurring on a frequent schedule, as I didn't want to be exposed to anything that could possibly be responsible for these Civil War dreams. Now that I was putting this whole project to an end, I felt that I could read any material of the Civil War. It is ironic that I just happened to open that book of 444 pages right to the page of that Confederate soldier's entry in his diary of an experience that seems to have so much in common with my dream.

Another entry of written documentation from that book caught my eye when a soldier wrote of the terrible marksmanship of the inexperienced soldier. He reported that many of the soldiers held their rifles at a 45 degree angle, and as a result the shots were fired way over the heads of the Yankees. This again reminds me of my dream in my chapter, "The Skirmish" when we purposely held our rifles at such high angles as to shoot over the heads of the Federal troops. As I continued to read I found other written documentation that seemed to parallel my own dream experiences. There is even a reference to my dream of the skirmish in the woods whereas they requested a temporary truce because they were low on food. I thought at first this dream was a little too unrealistic to be an actual past life memory, no matter how vivid and unforgettable it was. However, this book has an interesting bit of information that coincides with this dream. It states, "In Virginia in 1862, and in Mississippi the next year, informal truces were called to give soldiers opportunities to pick the luscious blackberries ripening on the no man's land that lay between the lines." I guess my dream was not so unrealistic after all.

Several weeks after my two additional dreams of the Civil War, I wrote to Dr. Holzer and told him of my new experiences in the Civil War, as I was sure he would be interested to know that almost three years after our hypnosis session the dreams are still occurring.

I never really discussed these dreams with anyone except for a few. It was apparent to me that what few family members and friends I confided in about these strange dreams had little reaction, and most of the impromptu flashbacks I kept to myself. Several years after the dream in 1978 of the funeral for our mule, I discussed it with a friend over lunch. I told her of the clarity of the details and the tremendous emotional impact it had on me, and how ridiculous I felt in the aftermath of that dream. I could not imagine crying so much over the death of a mule. She just listened to my story but made no comment.

I hardly mentioned these dreams to my brother as they occurred, but I did more so with my sister over coffee at her house. Since she had also experienced psychic dreams, I knew she would be more interested. With most of my other family members, such as my aunts, uncles or nieces, I remained silent. I didn't think they would really approve of my opinion of these dreams being a product of reincarnation. I also didn't want to risk being the object of joking remarks at our family gatherings and parties.

My sister eventually told her daughters of my book, and it seems my reluctance to tell them was unfounded. I was surprised when they told me they agreed that reincarnation is certainly a possibility. I believe the recent October 2000 TV movie, "Across Time and Death", which was about the Jenny Cockell story, may have convinced them even further.

I never mentioned the first two dreams to my coworkers, as again I didn't want to be ridiculed. These first two dreams occurred in 1978 while I was still working, and at that time I don't believe I was actually convinced it was reincarnation. I just thought they were two strange dreams that wouldn't stop haunting me. As I mentioned before, I thought hypnotic regression was the only way to experience a past life.

I never really made my past life dreams a topic of discussion with anyone except my pen pal, and of course, Dr. Hans Holzer as they occurred. My correspondence with Kristin began because of a mutual interest in parapsychology, so I was not embarrassed to write to her about these past life dream events. I guess other friends and family will just have to be shocked if they ever read of my experiences. People will believe what their education and life style dictate to them. All I know is that all of my flashbacks and dream experiences are true and unforgettable, right down to the last detail.

CHAPTER XXI

THE PERSISTENT FLASHBACKS

In the past few years, I have had nagging thoughts or memories of two past lives. To my knowledge, I have not dreamed nor have I seen in a movie the scenes that pervaded my thoughts almost on a daily basis. I see no reason to have these recurring thoughts, so therefore I'll have to consider them as past life flashbacks. The scene always starts the same way and ends the same way. They both deal with a different period in history, but I think the flashback that haunts me the most deals with my past life as a civilian long after the end of the Civil War.

The first recurring thought seems to take place in Medieval times. It is a very brief scene in which I am walking through a castle corridor with a group of young men and women. We are all dressed in typical medieval attire except we are all dressed in our finest clothes. The ladies are dressed in gowns and the men are wearing leotards, fancy shirts and vests. We all seem to be in our early twenties, except for the tall thin gentleman with the light brown hair and rather strange bowl haircut. He is walking in front of our group and he appears to be in his early thirties. The young lady I seem to be escorting is wearing a purple gown with large colorful sequins. She has short black wavy hair and a pretty face. She is about my height and appears to be a little on the heavy side.

As we walk through the corridor, the mood is a happy one, and I get the feeling we are on our way to a party. The castle walls in the corridor are white and the huge arch shaped windows on our right are located very high on the corridor wall. On our left is a concrete stairway trimmed with yellow paint. Straight ahead on the right is a room whose entrance is covered with a large green curtain. As we are walking and talking and laughing, we never reach that room.

Could this have been our final moments in that past life? Our mood was a happy one but perhaps there was an ominous threat to us all behind that green curtain. I can see no reason why this unusual thought would be so relentless, and why it decided to manifest only in the past few years.

The second flashback seems to take place in the very early part of the twentieth century. This scene is also very brief and constantly haunts my thoughts. I feel I am about 70 years of age and very tall and thin. I am dressed in a dark suit and standing at the top of a wide fancy stairway. The handrails are wide and polished. The wood is light like maplewood. The steps are covered with a beautiful red and blue designed carpet. I can see the lower level floor from the top of the stairway, and most of the decor seems to be various shades of brown. The front door has an oval shaped stained glass window, and the walls are covered with a brown pattern wallpaper. The curtains in the front windows are white and full. They appear to be crocheted.

My posture is ramrod straight but I feel so thin. I rest my hand on the handrail as I proceed to descend the staircase. I get as far as the third step and the flashback ends. The staircase seems to have about twenty steps. After many months of having this strange scenario creep into my thoughts, I had a dream. A vivid, colorful and unforgettable dream. The dream began when I was leaving my room at the end of the hall on the second floor in what appeared to be a hotel or boarding house. In the dream I was also very tall and thin and wearing a dark suit. I also felt I was about 70 years of age. I passed a series of doors on my right as I walked down the hallway, when suddenly I was almost hit in the face by a door as someone was leaving their room. I stopped quickly to avoid being struck by the door. I don't know why the doors to the rooms opened outward to the hall instead of inward. It seemed to be a real safety hazard. Perhaps this is the way hotel doors were hinged in those days, or a carpenter made an error.

At that moment two young women were leaving the room. One of them noticed me standing there and smiled a greeting. They were dressed in typical clothing for the early 1900's. Not only were they dressed alike, they even looked alike. I believe they were twins. They were beautiful young ladies with auburn hair rolled up in layers on their heads. They were wearing ankle length black pleated skirts and dark brown vests with a row of tiny buttons leading to their white frilled collars. They appeared to be about 21 years of age.

As they closed the door, they walked briskly ahead of me toward a staircase. They moved quickly and by the time I got to the staircase, they were out of sight. I rested my hand on the wide hand rail, and as I proceeded to descend I could see the same scenery as in my flashbacks. The front door with the oval stained glass and the white crocheted curtains. I got as far as the third step and I awoke! I didn't associate my surroundings with anything during the dream. It was when I awoke I realized I just dreamed about my continuous mental flashback.

I am now wondering if I may have survived the Civil War and spent my last days in a quaint but fancy boarding house. I was tall and very thin and about 70 years of age. Since I never seem to get past that third step on that stairway, I may have fallen and died in that house. These flashbacks have subsided lately. I wonder if I was being shown this series of thought flashbacks to prepare me for that dream, and also for an answer to my final destiny in that life.

At this time, I have not had a follow up dream of my stroll through the castle corridor with my friends. That mental flashback is still a mystery to me. I wonder if I was the same young man who was riding on that big white horse in the military procession through that hostile little village. The time frame could have been the same, as they both seem to take place in medieval times. However, one could live several lifetimes in that period of history, especially considering the relatively short life span of those times.

I still search for clues as to the meaning of this thought scenario. The castle appears bright and cheerful, not at all like a dark and damp dungeon atmosphere. We are all dressed up for a special occasion. Was I a friend or relative of a political or otherwise prominent person to be invited to such a gala affair in such a beautiful castle? These thoughts still haunt me occasionally, but not as often as before. Perhaps when I find a reason and an answer to their existence, they will fade away.

I feel I should mention another flashback that occurred to me in June 1996 as I was preparing to go to bed for the night. As I sat on the edge of the bed my eyes began to close and I suddenly found myself in a wooded area surrounded by Confederate soldiers milling about. I guess we were on a rest stop or about to set up camp for the rest of the day. While walking among the men, I saw a scurvy looking young man leaning against a tree holding his rifle by his side. This young fellow appeared to be about 17 years old, and looked as if he hadn't bathed or changed his clothes in years. He had dirty mussed blond hair and was obviously not wearing a uniform. His pants looked like burlap and were so filthy dirty I don't know whether the dark green was the actual color of his pants or if they were covered with moss and mildew. They appeared to be tightly bound around his skinny waist with a rope. He also wore a dirty shirt and vest. He looked as if he hadn't eaten in months.

I was about 8 feet from him as we looked at each other. We didn't speak but he stood there sneering at me. I definitely got the impression he didn't like me. As I started to walk away, I noticed a remarkable contrast in his attire. As I looked down I could see he was wearing the most expensive and fancy looking boots I have ever seen. They were obviously not government issued but more like something a rich Texas cattle baron would wear on his ranch. They were clean light brown leather and covered with an intricate gold swirl design. These boots must have been a recent addition to his wardrobe, as I could see they looked new.

How this unkempt and dirty young man acquired these boots was a mystery to me. I'm sure he didn't have the money to pay for such an expensive luxury item. If he stole them, it must have been from a wealthy civilian, perhaps before he joined the Confederate Army. I don't know why he wasn't wearing a uniform. As his youth would indicate, he may have been a new recruit and had not as yet been issued one. As I walked away from him the flashback ended. I'm sure this whole experience only lasted perhaps a minute or two and I was still sitting on the edge of the bed.

He has been on my mind so much these past few months I thought I had better include him. It's as if this "ghost" from the past knows I forgot to include him in my book and he has come back to haunt me.

I am still often confronted in my thoughts by this young sneering soldier standing in front of me while wearing his expensive boots. It seems these sudden jolts into the past are like burning yourself on a hot stove. The experience is very brief but the resulting scar lasts forever.

During this same time period I had more unusual paranormal experiences unrelated to past lives. I wrote about them in an article that appeared in Fate magazine on November 1999.

****

THE GHOSTS OF HAMILTON SQUARE

It was around 6:00pm on a summer day in 1997 when my brother and I approached a red traffic light. It was a busy place where two main highways intersect in the quiet town of Hamilton Square, a suburb of Trenton, New Jersey. On the right was a bank and various small businesses. On the left was a small, triangular, grassy island bout 40 by 60 feet. As we waited at a red light, I observed a young woman standing on the island near the curb. She appeared to be wearing a very old-fashioned beige and white nurse's uniform with the insignia of the Red Cross. At first I assumed she was taking up a collection for a hospital or other medical charity, but as I watched her I could see that she had no collection paraphernalia, not even a little sign.

She was of medium height and weight with short, wavy brown hair and dark brown eyes. She appeared to be about 30 years old. Her face was tan from the sun. She made no attempt to cross the street and she wasn't hitchhiking. As I watched her she made no attempt at eye contact with any of the drivers who were waiting for the light to change. She even seemed oblivious to all the cars around her as she stood there with a very contented smile on her pretty face. As I sat in the front passenger's seat, I looked around at the other drivers. It seemed that everyone was looking straight ahead at the traffic light. Did anyone other than my brother and I even see her?

My brother later referred to her as the "World War I nurse", and as I looked through old photos in books, I believe her ankle-length uniform could have been from that era. That contented expression on her face while standing in the middle of a busy intersection and wearing an 80-year-old nurse's uniform led me to believe she was possibly an escaped mental patient. However, I now believe she was a ghost who perhaps died on that very spot many years ago.

My trips to the library and bookstores in search of information regarding this place in that era were fruitless but an old neighbor told me that the area where the bank now stands was once a farmhouse. Could this nurse have been the wife or daughter of the farmer who lived there and perhaps died an accidental death near the farmhouse? A great influenza epidemic followed the closing months of World War I. Perhaps she was one of the victims of this deadly disease while caring for someone else who was afflicted.

Another strange sighting occurred on a sunny winter afternoon around 4:00pm on February 2, 1998. This was also about a mile from my house along a narrow stretch of road in a residential neighborhood. There are no traffic lights on this road but the speed limit is only 25 miles per hour.

As my brother and I approached a small bridge that crosses a creek, we suddenly saw a policeman perched on his motorcycle on a dirt path just off the right side of the road. He had backed the motorcycle along the trees by the bridge and the creek so that he was facing the road, ready for a hot pursuit. I immediately took my foot off the gas to lower my speed, because he looked like he meant business. As we drove by, we were astonished to see he was wearing an old-fashioned dark blue uniform with flared trousers. He appeared to be wearing knee-high boots, but I distinctly remember mud on his left shoe. He was a heavyset man with a short, thick mustache. He wore goggles and a dark blue hat with a black peak. He was sitting on an antique motorcycle.

He looked like something you would see on the cover of a 1926 *Saturday Evening Post* magazine, hiding behind a highway billboard. We were on our way to Atlantic City that day and all the way I couldn't get that unusual sight out of my mind. It wasn't until we stopped to eat that something occurred to me. Why was that policeman wearing such a strange and outdated uniform? And why in the world was he sitting on an antique motorcycle?

On our was back home, it was late at night and I was anxious to see once again the spot where we had seen the policeman. Much to my surprise, there was no dirt path in that spot. Trees and bushes bordered a paved driveway belonging to the house next to the creek, and yet I was sure I had seen his motorcycle parked on a dirt path. This only added to the mystery, because a motorcycle policeman wouldn't park in someone's driveway while waiting for speeders.

Could it be he was a ghost who died in the line of duty on that spot more that 70 years ago? It's strange that both the nurse and the cop were wearing uniforms of about the same era. And if they both were ghosts, wasn't it unusual for both my brother and I to be able to see them? I wrote to the famous author on ghosts, Dr. Hans Holzer, and presented this question to him after giving him a detailed description of our sightings. His reply was that two people who are close sometimes do have that experience together. He also suggested that I try taking photos of these areas. He told me that I am psychic and that something might show up.

In a photo of the site where the nurse stood, a strange

arc of light appears. A picture of the area only several feet away and taken about a second later shows nothing out of the ordinary. At one time, I had taken a photo of this place using a different camera and a different brand of film, and the arc of light was still visible on the developed film on that frame. This does not necessarily prove an spiritual presence at this location, but I am at a loss for an explanation of why this arc of light keeps showing up on three different rolls of film.

Could she still be haunting that place, oblivious to all the changes that have taken place over the decades? The serene and contented expression on her face seems to indicate that she is happy. Perhaps in her own dimension, she is standing in her front yard enjoying the flowers and fresh air. Every time I have to stop at that red light, I look for her and say a silent "hello". I also look for the motorcycle cop. Although I have only seen them once, both he and the nurse were sights I will never forget.

****

Maybe all these experiences are somehow related: the reliving of scenes from my past lives and glimpses of entities from bygone times. Maybe the veil that separates the present and the past is thinning and is allowing me temporary access. The problem is that these events cannot be predicted or controlled.

CHAPTER XXII

THE DREAMS CONTINUE

It had been many months since my dream of the temporary truce in the woods and my search for food. I had been spending some time keeping in touch with Kristin, my pen pal in Salt Lake City, and updating and preparing my journal of all my past life dreams of the Civil War. Several months ago I was introduced through the mail to Pam, another pen pal of Kristin from Tucson, Arizona. She is an enthusiastic Civil War buff, which is how we began to correspond. Kristin shared some of my dream experiences I had written to her with Pam, and her interest and curiosity in my unusual dreams along with her love of Civil War history prompted her to write to me. It has been my pleasure to correspond with both of these women and share our interests and dreams.

About a month ago I had another sequence of dreams of the past. However, these dreams didn't take place on a battlefield, and I wasn't running from or shooting at the Federal troops. It seemed to take place in a time before the Civil War, as I seemed quite young. The first night I dreamed I was standing on a dirt road looking out at a huge farm. The sky was hazy and a misty fog blanketed the woods on the horizon. I don't know whether it was early morning or late afternoon, but the sun wasn't shining and the fog and mist gave the whole scene a depressing atmosphere. A row of tall trees extended out onto the field, and since they were full of green foliage, it may have been late spring or summer.

As I stood at the edge of the road looking out at the farm land, I heard the sound of horse's hooves. I could see a man driving a big horse drawn wagon approaching me from my left. As he got closer I could see the driver perched high on a wooden seat. He was a young man perhaps in his middle 20's and wore a long sleeve blue and red checkered shirt and a wide brim gray hat. He was smiling as he pulled the wagon over behind me and stopped to talk for a few minutes.

His wagon was very large with big spoked wooden wheels. It was carrying a full load of what appeared to be a ground up mixture of yellow, green and brown vegetation which I assume was compost. I don't remember what we talked about but I felt that I knew him. Perhaps our discussion was about the farm, as we both seemed to be staring out at that field as we talked. I don't know how old I was but I seemed to be quite young, perhaps in my early teens. I was leaning against the front wagon wheel staring out at that field and listening to the driver talking when I awoke.

That dream stuck in my mind all day. It seemed to be like a film clip being shown over and over in my mind and I knew this must have been another past life memory. Perhaps this was a small part of my young life before the Civil War. I don't know whether I lived on this big farm or was just passing by as a neighbor who lived nearby. I did seem to be quite friendly with the wagon driver, so I don't think I was a stranger in the area.

The following night I had a surprise in store. As I fell asleep I dreamed I was walking around the classroom of an old one room schoolhouse. Either school was closed or class was recessed for the day, as I was alone. I was looking at the students' desks and other items of interest, and I noticed the teacher's big wooden desk was situated on a low platform next to the front door. A big coal stove stood against the wall near a window in the center of the room. Everything in that room seemed to have been made rather crudely, including the wooden floor and the windows.

Even though the windows were small, there appeared to be enough of them to have offered more outside light than they did, as it was quite dark inside. There seemed to be about eight windows all together, four on each side of the room. I walked over to the window to see outside and there before me was that same field I was looking at in my dream the night before. There was even some mist forming on the horizon again. At this moment I awoke.

It was so odd that I dreamed of the same area two nights in a row but from two different locations. In the first dream of the wagon driver, I was not aware of a schoolhouse in the nearby vicinity. My attention was directed at the field in front of me, but the schoolhouse was probably located behind me on the other side of the road. Perhaps this was my usual walk from school, passing by the big farm field on my way home. The dimly lit school room in my dream made me wonder about the ability to offer enough light in those little school houses in those early days to read and teach. After all, they couldn't just turn on a wall switch and light up the room with ceiling florescent lights. You couldn't rely on the bright sunshine to offer enough light through the windows, especially on the dark and cloudy days of winter. Were kerosene lamps used in the daytime in schools? I never gave this problem a thought until this dream had me roaming around that small dark classroom. I don't know why I was hanging around that schoolhouse after hours. It almost seemed like I came back to visit the place.

Apparently, that was not the last dream of that past life childhood. The following week I had another dream of walking across a narrow stretch of plowed field that was flanked by a patch of woods on both sides. I seemed to be about 11 years old and was accompanied by another boy who seemed perhaps a year or two older and a head taller than I. We were both wearing overalls and he was wearing a green and red polka dot shirt with no collar. As we trudged across the dirt clods 1 suddenly became extremely agitated. It seemed to be about something the other boy was eating, and I started shouting at him and began punching him. Perhaps he stole my snack, although I probably would have shared it with him anyway if I were older. My punches to his face and chest didn't seem to faze him, as he did a pretty good job of deflecting my punches. We were still fighting as I awoke.

I thought it very strange that my dreams seemed to be regressing to my childhood of my past life before the Civil War. All of these dreams seemed to occur on farm land, and I spent my childhood in this lifetime living in apartment buildings in the city. Even the clothing we wore in my last childhood dream seemed to be of a preCivil War era. I felt so bad about hitting that boy in my dream when I awoke, even though I didn't seem to be hurting him. In fact, he was smiling and smirking at me all the while. Perhaps he was my older brother who liked to agitate me, as older brothers at that age often do. Perhaps that only added to my frustration in my temper outburst. He was taller and older than I and I had to reach up to try to make contact with my fist. Although I was never involved in fist fights in my childhood in this lifetime, I guess it always was pretty much a normal part of growing up.

About two months had gone by since the dream of my childhood fight on the farm. One afternoon I was sitting on the sofa in my living room reading a recent letter I received from Kristin. It was now May of 1997, and in the blink of an eye I experienced another "flashback." Suddenly, I was sitting on the edge of a white cot in a tent wearing my gray long johns. It was night time and I could see through the open flap door of the tent that a Confederate soldier was guarding the entrance to the tent. He was a big broad shouldered man wearing a tan uniform with a wide strap across his chest. He appeared to be on high alert, as he seemed very rigid and tense. As I sat on the edge of the cot, I noticed a small wooden folding table near the entrance to the tent. It contained three books stacked up (the middle one was very thick with gilded edged pages). A rolled up map lay alongside the books, and a canteen with a light blue cover was lying on top of the pile of books.

The side of the cot I was sitting on was facing toward the center of the tent, and I had to crane my neck to look out the open flap door. There was a lot of tension in the air as I strained my eyes to see past the guard and into the darkness. I was watching the silhouette of the bushes and trees that surrounded our tent, as if I were anticipating something to happen. The guard still stood stationary and he was still clutching his rifle closely to his chest. I was vaguely aware of another cot in the tent. It was situated along the right wall of the tent, several feet from the wooden folding table. The cot I was sitting on was located along the wall of the front of the tent. The cots were only accessible from one side, as the other side of the cot was so close to the wall of the tent.

My anxiety concerning the activity outside the tent resulted in my being unaware of the details inside the tent. The tent seemed rather large as compared to a soldier's pup tent. Was I in a hospital tent for the sick and wounded? It reminded me of the officers' quarters, especially with room for several cots and a table and a guard posted at the entrance. I don't know why I remained seated on the edge of that cot if I was so intensely interested in looking out the flap door. As I kept a watchful vigil I suddenly found myself back on my living room sofa with Kristin's letter in my lap.

It was unfortunate that I didn't sit on the cot and observe the whole interior of the tent, but I have no control over these strange visits to the past. I don't know why I was sitting on the edge of the cot. Perhaps a disturbance outside awoke me and I was just sitting up from a sound sleep. I call this experience a "flashback" because it came on so quickly, and even though the description of what I saw and experienced seemed like a lot of time involved, I'm sure the whole experience was probably over in less than a minute. As I mentioned to Kristin in relating this latest experience, I hope these flashbacks don't occur at inopportune times, such as while I'm driving a car. So far they seem to occur while I'm relaxing and reading. Perhaps relaxation is the key to opening the door to the subconscious.

Since all of these dreams are still so vivid in my memory, I am always on the prowl for books that may possibly shed some light on some of the sights and scenery of these dreams. I have been fortunate to find an illustration of the types of uniforms worn by both the North and the South. While browsing through a book store at the mall, I was delighted to see among the illustrated army of the Confederacy a general wearing the chapeau worn by General Sam McGowan in my dream. I at first thought this type of hat was worn only by the Union officers because of the book of antiques I referred to earlier. It stated they were U.S. Government issued. Apparently, these strange looking hats were worn more by the Confederates, so probably the government issue I referred to previously meant the Confederate government. I have not seen this type of hat worn by the

Union officers.

I became skeptical of several items in this flashback of the tent. For example, the canteen that lay on top of the pile of books was covered with light blue cloth. I did not think canteen covers existed in those days, but again I saw a recent color photo in a book of a cloth covered canteen used during the Civil War. The cloth was full of holes from age but it was the same shade of light blue as the one I saw on the pile of books. The second item in that tent I had my doubts about was the invention of a folding table. Again, I was surprised to see the same table in General Lee's tent in a painting by Mort Kunstler in his book of the South. It was even located in exactly the same spot in his tent near the entrance.

I could never forget that unusual tree General McGowan was standing next to in my dream. I have never seen one like it in this lifetime, with its thick trunk and low gnarled horizontal twisted branches. It was only recently that I came across a book titled, *North American Trees* by Barbara Burn. As I browsed through it I saw the tree that looked like the one in my dream. It was a pecan tree, which is grown throughout the South. I bought the book and made several copies of that pecan tree and sent them to my pen pals, as they knew of my dream of General McGowan.

The timing was right because Pam let me know she was going to be taking a vacation to visit the Civil War sites in Pennsylvania, Virginia and Maryland, and she told me she would keep her eyes open for such a tree in her travels. I thought it may offer a clue as to where I was that day on the battlefield. It even crossed my mind that the dry light brown dirt that covered General McGowan's uniform as he struggled to get to his feet may have been a dry pecan shell residue. However, I know nothing about pecan trees and it was just a thought.

When Pam returned from her visit to the Civil War

battle grounds, she found some interesting information for me. One of her excursions took her to a place called Fisher's Hill in Orange, Virginia. There she followed a Confederate path which led to a softly sloping hill where a battle once took place. She told me it was at the very summit of the hill she saw the same tree as the photo copy I sent to her. Pam had also learned from reading a book at her place of lodging that General Samuel McGowan's Brigade had joined Jeb Stuart at a place called Liberty Mills in Orange in late January of 1864.

If my dream took place in this area in the Spring of 1864, General McGowan's left leg wound would have been a year old, and as witnessed by physician's notes from the Archives, he never seemed to really recuperate from that leg wound. This would explain his apparent damage to his left leg without the obvious blood. Of course, pecan trees are probably quite abundant throughout the South, but it is such a coincidence that Pam's visit to that little town connected a tree and a general in my dream at the same place.

Another copy I made was of a photo of an incredible likeness of that bridge in my dream. The photo was in a book called, *The Civil War Trust's Official Guide to the Civil War Discovery Trail* by Frommer. The photo was taken at the Mine Creek Battlefield State Historic Site at Pleasonton, Kansas. I don't believe I was in Kansas that night as we carried those kegs of gunpowder through the high weeds, but the architectural design of the bridge in the photo is almost identical to the one in my dream. The only difference is the position of the guard rail beam. In the photo the beam appears to be attached at the sides or the narrow edge of the beam. In my dream the guard rail was attached on the flat surface of the beam. The bridge in the photo even appears to be arched and tapers down to the ground. This is the only photo I have ever seen of a bridge that looks so much like the one in my dream. Perhaps it was a common architectural design at that time.

Pam also mentioned that there were many covered bridges in the vicinity of Orange, Virginia. The bridge she made mention of crossed the Rapidan River. Although the bridge in my dream was not a covered bridge, its possible a cover was built for it in later years. Her information was very interesting and helpful. I have never heard of Orange, Virginia, but a visit there just may conjure up some flashbacks or memories.

These dreams of past lives, especially those dreams of the Civil War will always be with me. I suppose I'll be spending the rest of my life searching for familiar places to hopefully someday find a clue as to my identity in the Civil War. Perhaps if these dreams continue, names and places will be mentioned that will be beneficial to this quest.

These past life dreams have also made me realize how insignificant, and yet how much emphasis people place on physical beauty. If these dreams truly represent a memory of a past existence, my soul has found a home in many human shapes and sizes. The important principle is how we think and conduct our behavior toward others. Our bodies, as miraculous and versatile as they may be, are just temporary shells that we rely on to function in this world, but I believe the soul lives on forever.

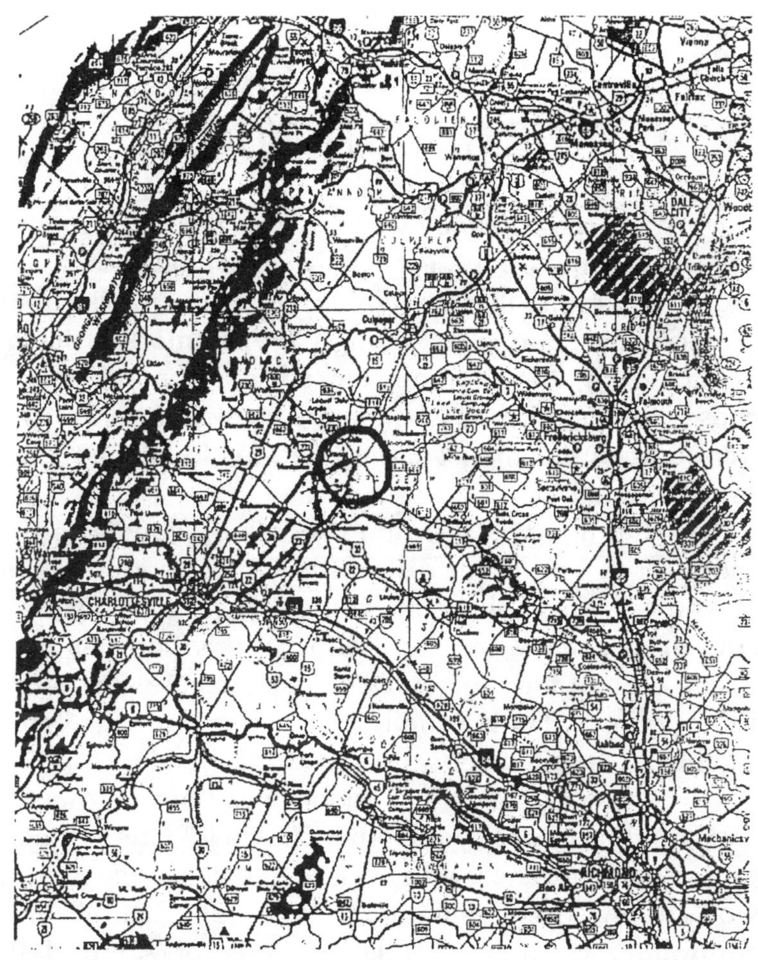

The circled area is Orange, the place where my pen pal visited and reported seeing a pecan tree like the one I described to her from my dream. It is also the same area where General Sam McGowan camped and fought.

CHAPTER XXIII

THE ILLUSTRATIONS

Many readers may wonder how the illustrations in this book came about, especially since I didn't do the art work. After all, these were my dream and flashback experiences, and even though the memories still are crystal clear, they remain locked in my mind. Having these illustrations published in this book became such an intriguing and complex affair, I decided to let the readers in on the details.

While I was still in the process of working on my manuscript I met an artist at the Quakerbridge Mall in Lawrenceville, a suburb of Trenton, N.J. Twice a year he sets up a shed where he hangs up his portraits in an inside area of the mall outside the stores and just off the thoroughfare. He is usually there several weeks before Mother's Day as well as the Christmas holidays.

The artist, Morris E. Docktor, was born on May 20, 1948 in the city of Philadelphia, Pa. He told me his talent and visual awareness was evident at a very early age. He won many art competitions in High School, then continued to study at Tyler College of Art and the Pennsylvania Academy of the Fine Arts. His studies precipitated worldwide travel. Morris is continually fulfilling mural, portrait and sculpture commissions. His art work is represented in museums and in many important collections.

Morris is a charismatic and worldly man whose youthful appearance belies his thirty plus years experience as an accomplished artist. Many times during his visit to the mall we would talk about our individual ideas of life and we would often discuss our past experiences. I was often intrigued as I watched him work at his easel. I have seen him work only with photographs at the mall, but perhaps he has had some of his subjects pose for him at his studio on occasion. I was particularly fascinated how he is always able to duplicate a facial expression. Whether the photo of the subject has a warm and sincere smile or an insincere attempt at a smile, it will show in the portrait. A smile isn't just a smile with Morris. He shows the true personality of the subject as reflected in the photo.

During one of his visits to the mall, he told me of a project he had once completed for an author. It was then I finally told him of the book I was writing. I thought he might be a little skeptical about the subject of reincarnation, so I had never mentioned it. As I described some of my dreams and flashbacks, he listened intently. I think he was wondering how I could describe a dream I had so long ago with such minute detail. Even the weather conditions during these dreams remained a part of the experiences.

After I finished talking and reliving some of these past life dreams, he told me a few illustrations would really add some additional interest to my book. I had never thought about that before. There were indeed a few past life scenes of the Civil War that seemed to haunt my memory more than the others. Morris said he could do the illustrations for my book if I chose to have them done. I became captivated with the idea but at that time I still had some work to do on my book, and of course, I was still looking for a publisher. I told him if I found someone to publish my book when it is completed, I would take his advice and see what he could do. Even though the last flashback at that time took place two years before in May 1997, all of these dreams and flashbacks were still very vivid in my memory, but that is

where they remained. I have always seen Morris work from photographs
but I couldn't give him a photo of my thoughts.

While I was in the process of putting some finalized information on my book, I was also in correspondence with Ozark Mountain Publishing, Inc., who expressed an interest in my book. I mentioned to them that I would like to have a few illustrations inserted in strategic chapters of my book. I told them of my association with Morris and that he was very experienced in his work. I was told that the illustrations would be up to me, but they must be approved by the publisher before being printed.

It was in February of 2001 that a contract consummated my association with the publisher. I was told the printer would not be able to start on my book until late in the year, so I still had time to add some information to my book. Once I was sure I was satisfied that my writing was done, I was anxious to contact Morris again. The last time we spoke of his doing my illustrations was during his visit to the mall during the 2000 Christmas holidays. At that time we had agreed to go forward with the pictures, but he said he wanted to take some photos of the trees and shrubs and fields. Apparently, he still preferred to work from photos, but I agreed this was a good idea. We discussed this project and decided to meet again on his next visit to the mall in early May in anticipation of his doing portraits for Mother's Day. I told him that would be best because by then the leaves will be growing once again on the trees. Since my two chosen pictures at that time seemed to take place in May and July, judging by the green foliage and the weather conditions, we decided to meet in May.

I wasn't sure if Morris could really capture the whole scene that has been haunting my thoughts all these years just by my description. I bought a sketch pad and pencils and tried to draw what has been locked in my thoughts since 1978. 1 am not an artist but I was successful in drawing the scene of that Federal trooper aiming his rifle at my face while I was attempting to rescue my wounded comrade. Also, the scene of General Sam McGowan standing under that pecan tree and the young Federal troops exiting the woods in the background was presentable. At least by my amateur drawings, Morris could now see the location of the woods and the body positions.

As we discussed my sketches, I realized he was even more particular with minute details than I was, which pleased me very much. He even asked me the approximate time of day so he would know how to arrange the shadows. I had a good feeling about our discussion of my sketches and that he knew exactly what I expected. I would never be satisfied if these haunting memories were missing even the slightest detail. I also supplied him with some of the Civil War reference books I purchased so he could be more acquainted with the weapons and uniforms. When I mentioned how tall and thin I was in those dreams, he told me that described a friend of his, even down to the straight black hair. I asked Morris if he would ask his friend to accompany us on our photo journey in the spring. As long as he is taking photos of the woods and fields, why not ask his friend to strike a few poses for us. Since the Christmas holiday was over and Morris was leaving the mall, I told him I would see him in May when he returned.

As the winter months passed and spring arrived, I saw his artist shed erected and locked waiting for his return. It was Sunday April 29th and he was expected to return the next day. The following morning I saw him setting up his easel and hanging his portraits. I had so many questions and ideas I wanted to discuss and confirm with him. I also worried a bit that he may have committed himself to so many projects over the past few months, he might have to hold off on our book project. Even though I was told my book would not be printed until late in the year, I wanted the publisher to have the illustrations no later than the beginning of July. After all, I still needed their approval on the art work.

We talked as he set up his work place and the first question I asked him was about his tall thin friend. Did he ask him to accompany us and pose for our photo session, or perhaps he was too busy and had no interest in the whole project? The answer was an enthusiastic yes! He would be glad to join us on our photo odyssey. Morris told me he was committed to working three weeks at the mall and as soon as his time was through, we would meet at the mall with his friend and look for the closest resemblance of the wooded terrain in my dreams. At the time, the trees were still budding and not quite in full bloom, so the whole arrangement and timing sounded good. I had typed a quotation from the text to be placed under each photo of the picture before it was to be sent to the publisher.

Some of the selections of mental pictures took place at night and I assumed they would be too much of a challenge for Morris, especially since they would be done in charcoal. However, he told me he thought he could portray a night scene with enough visual clarity. I told him of the scene I would like to see recreated from my chapter, "The Campsite." it was not only night time, it was also lightly raining. I guess our lanterns threw off enough light to partially illuminate the end of the street where we were camped, because the other end of the street was in total darkness. I explained to Morris what type of buildings were located on both sides of the street.

When I went home from the mall, I picked up my sketch pad and pencil once again and tried to draw that night scene of the street in that little town. I had a lot of difficulty with the alignment of the buildings but eventually, it all started to come together. This dream had also always been a haunting memory and I would be very pleased if Morris could arrange this whole street scene for me. The next day, I brought my drawing with me to the mall to give Morris the visual effect I was seeking. I managed to give an accurate representation of the business side of the street as well as a depiction of the wooden shanty houses with the porch railings on the right side of the street. The sky was not pitch black and the lanterns gave off enough light to see as far as my picture indicated. Morris studied my drawing and seemed confident he could do what I was asking.

I suddenly remembered an old Civil War rifle I bought at a antique collectible show at the mall in Cherry Hill, N.J. back in the early 1980's. It had been residing in my attic and I told Morris about it. It is an 1853 Enfield rifle with a ramrod and in very good condition for its age. It is four and a half feet long and very heavy. Even though it can be used to this day with the powder and proper ammo, in this lifetime I wouldn't have a clue how to load it. Carrying this type of weapon around with me everywhere was routine in my dreams and flashbacks of the Civil War, and yet in this lifetime it is just an old harmless antique to me.

I guess I had a strong pair of arms and shoulders to carry this big rifle everywhere we walked and ran. It would be such an irony if this rifle was actually the same one I used in that past lifetime. Of course, I'll never know. Morris became very interested in it and asked me to bring it with me for the photo episode.

We met at the Quakerbridge Mall the day after Memorial Day near noon. Morris told me he couldn't reach his tall thin friend for the photo shoot, so we decided to do it ourselves. Morris is athletic and trim and about 6 feet tall, so the body seemed close enough, even though he is not a 6'5" stringbean as I once was. Also, instead of using the park areas in Princeton, N.J., he decided to take the photos on his property. He had 11 acres and most of it was woods and fields. I felt more at ease with this new arrangement because we would be doing a lot of posing with my old rifle and I felt more comfortable having the privacy of his private property.

The journey to his home in Pennington, N.J. seemed to me to be a confusing mass of noon time traffic which eventually led to several back country roads. I was relieved when I asked him to take me in his car instead of my driving and meeting him there. This was an area I was not familiar with at all and I would have gotten lost for sure. As we drove into his driveway, I was impressed by the unique design of his home. Morris told me he had designed it himself and it has been featured in national publications and is considered an architectual landmark. When we entered his home he gathered some clothing he thought we could wear: a long sleeve shirt, a vest and a sport coat jacket, which we pinned at the top to resemble as close as possible the jackets worn by the soldiers in those days. We wanted to simulate the attire worn by the people in my dreams close enough to photograph the wrinkles in the clothing during the poses. Morris even donned a pair of knee high boots which clearly represented the boots we wore.

As we walked out his living room glass door, I was very impressed with his outdoor decor. His patio porch area was shaded by trees and a lily pond was a nice attraction located only a few feet from his patio. I looked out upon the field and trees and saw a gazebo at the head of a beautiful fountain the size of a swimming pool. With my heavy old rifle and his telescopic camera, we set out across the lawn that led us beyond the bushes to a huge field and rows of trees. As I looked around I knew we had come very close to the scenery I needed. The sun was barely poking through the clouds and we wished the sky would clear enough to let the sun give us the clarity and shadows we wanted.

Morris was already aware of the scenery we tried to create with our body positions, and we took turns taking pictures of each other and exchanging the long sleeve shirt and vest or the coat and the rifle. He had already seen and still had the drawings I did of these particular scenes, so he knew exactly where to stand and how to pose with very little direction from me. I became General McGowan while I was wearing the sport coat. I tried to give it a discheveled look by bending and twisting my body before Morris took my photo. The general appeared this way to me when he finally was able to get back on his feet. I also posed bending and arching my left leg and leaning more on my right leg. I also became the wounded comrade lying on the ground near the bush after I donned the white long sleeve shirt and vest. We took turns becoming the Union soldiers running from the woods while carrying my old rifle with two hands in a fixed bayonet position.

Eventually, Morris told me we had to take a break while he changed the roll of film in his camera. Suddenly, he realized the aperture was not set according to the speed of the film. He said we would have to do the whole sequence of scenes again. Just as he was putting a new roll of film in the camera, the sun shone brightly as the clouds moved away. These were the weather conditions we wanted in the first place. Morris gave me some quick instructions on how to use the camera but I didn't trust my results due to my confusion with the focus and the telescopic device on the camera. As soon as Morris put in a new role of film, we repeated all of our previous scenes with the sun shining. Also, by this time I knew how to operate the camera. I think it was a blessing that we had to do the whole photo shoot over again.

As we headed to his house, he told me he had a raincoat that might look like the one I described and drew in my campsite scene. When he came out wearing the raincoat I handed him the rifle and he stood with his back to me. I took his picture and it gave me such a chill to see him as I was in the dream, wearing the boots and raincoat and holding the rifle by his side in his left hand. I wasn't sure about taking the picture in shade but he told me it was night time in my dream so it would be alright. Of course, these props as well as our bodies and the scenery were only a guide to the actual illustrations.

Several days after the photo session, I began to wonder if there were any important details that I forgot to mention or just didn't emphasize enough. To put my mind at ease, I wrote several details concerning each of the three pictures in a letter to Morris.

Four weeks went by before I heard from Morris. We were to meet again at the mall where he would show me the three basic sketches. I was glad I could still tell him if a few minor changes had to be made before the finished product.

At last the much awaited day arrived and we met on a Monday evening at Quakerbridge Mall. Along with the three sketches, he had an envelope full of photos that we took on his property. I wondered why he had so many of these photos of our Civil War poses. I assumed he discarded the first roll that he thought was defective. Even though some of them were a little blurred, it was a surprise that most of them came out clear anyway. Apparently, we didn't need to repeat that whole sequence of poses for the second role of film, but at least we had the sun shining for us the second time around.

As he laid out the drawings we discussed them one by one. Except for a very few minor suggestions of changes, I was very pleased. He knew exactly what scenes to portray as evidenced by the three sketches that lay before me. They were a little rough at this stage as expected, but I knew he would be ready to send the photos of the finished product to the publisher in a few weeks. I was glad to see that Morris met the challenge of such an unusual assignment with such success.

This art project has been a deviation from Morris' usual routine and I am sure it is one he will never forget. It is certainly different from someone handing you a photograph at the mall and attaching it to your easel while you work on the portrait. To go to all the trouble of having our long discussions on the details of these pictures, as well as taking me to his property where he became photographer and actor for this project, really illustrates his determination to create the most accurate work of art for my book. Needless to say, I will always be grateful for his patience and dedication.

At least a few of these haunting dream images were at last made available for other people to see. While most people have memories of their childhood and early youth, they are restricted to remembering events only of their present lifetime. Thoughts of events of my past lives manage to infiltrate my mind almost on a daily basis, and sometimes they will linger throughout the day. I can't tell you how often I have ridden on that big white horse through that medieval village of hostile residents, or lay on that field in "The Carnage" and watched the stars while listening to the delirium of the other wounded soldiers. Of course, that short interrupted walk down that staircase in the old victorian style hotel never ceases to haunt my thoughts.

This is a true story that I believe needed to be told, and I'm thankful for the opportunity to share this experience with you.

THE END

EPILOGUE

When it was first suggested to me that I should write a book about these past life dreams, I really thought I didn't have enough material to accomplish this project. Some of my dreams were quite brief and their content sometimes quite unusual. If I were writing a fiction novel there would have been no problem to write a lengthy story, and perhaps change the content or even the ending of my dreams to make them either more interesting or at least more feasible.

I could have added many more dreams to my story that I never really experienced to make my story more compelling. After all, these past life dreams occurred only to me, so who would know the difference? Well, the truth is I would know the difference. To alter these dream experiences in any way in this book would not only be morally unethical, it would be a sacrilege to me, as I consider the experience of these past life dreams almost a "religious" experience.

I have always had an open mind about reincarnation, just as I have an open mind about the existence of UFO's, ghosts and other paranormal events that have been written about so often. Reincarnation to me always seemed a possibility but never a proven fact. As these dream experiences have demonstrated to me, even though I have no actual proof of having lived and fought during the Civil War, there is still plenty of evidence to support my previous existence.

One final example of this evidence manifested on my recent visit to the Civil War re-enactment, which occurs annually at our local park. As I first entered the park, tents were erected where souvenirs were sold. Just outside the visitor's tents was a table that held a rifle and other Civil War items. As I got closer to examine the rifle, I saw several of those strange looking bullets that had small sacks attached. A man came over to me and asked if I had any questions. I asked him how the rifle was loaded. When he opened the breech and reached for bullets, I realized this was the same type of rifle and ammo I was loading in my dream. In the dream, I was inserting one bullet after the other in the chamber. I asked him how many bullets this rifle held and he told me it held 14 bullets.

My legs started to get weak with excitement. I saw samples of these bullets last year in the last re-enactment, but I never saw the rifle along with the bullets before. As he demonstrated the loading procedure for me, the whole dream flashed before me of hiding in those high weeds on that hill just outside the woods, with that rifle laying at my feet. I started to feel a little weak and thought I had better sit for a minute. There is no way in this lifetime I would ever have any idea that such a rifle that carried those strange looking bullets ever existed. This was truly evidence of that past lifetime to me.

I soon walked toward the Confederate camp and began to mingle with the men dressed in their Confederate attire. I let several of them know I was having a book published and even distributed a copy of a one page description of the essence of my book and why I decided to write it. Two of the men I approached from the start were very friendly and helpful.

I told them of several of my vivid dreams and let them know I still had questions. When I told them of the strange looking hat one of them was wearing in the dream of the bridge, they brought forth several hats to show me. I explained in detail several times the hat in my dream, but the hats they were showing me were not the same. I almost felt they were trying to trick me into changing my description by showing me the same style hat again. Finally, it became apparent to one of the men that the hat I described was called a "plantation hat". The extra wide brim protected the eyes from the sun while working in the field.

I also told them of my last flashback of sitting on the cot in the tent at night while a guard stood outside the open flap. I explained that there seemed to be some activity going on in camp at that time, and I didn't know why a guard was stationed by me. For some unknown reason the two men asked me how the guard was holding his rifle. They struck several poses while holding their rifles in various positions while asking me if this was the way he looked. I told them none of the poses matched the guard. I asked one of the men for his rifle and I showed them how the guard looked.

As he handed me the rifle, I grasped it with both hands closely together. While clutching the rifle tightly around the stock and barrel in an upright position, I stood at attention with the barrel pressed against my chest. The man whose rifle I borrowed exclaimed in a surprised reaction that this was a special salute that is only presented to high ranking officials. It was then I began to wonder if the commotion in camp that night was due to a surprise visit from a general or other high ranking official. It was difficult to see past the guard that night, and all I could see was the silhouette of the trees and bushes and a few soldiers whose faces were illuminated by the camp fire. I still don't know why that guard was stationed there at my tent, but I learned something about the way he was carrying his rifle while standing at attention. Both of these men were very interesting to talk with and very helpful in my search for answers to the events that occurred in those Civil War dreams.

To this day these dream experiences haunt me and follow me every day like a shadow. The experience that seems to haunt me the most is that skirmish in the woods. The entire scene is constantly being replayed in my mind. I guess when someone aims a rifle at your face, whether it happened last week or 140 years ago, it's something you don't forget.

I told Dr. Holzer before the hypnosis that I wanted to try to remember as much as I could about my past life, and to retain those memories when the hypnosis session had come to an end. Apparently I got my wish, but I have not regrets. Although I would have liked to remember my identity so that this previous life could be confirmed, I am still convinced that these dreams were not just self induced fantasy. To learn as much as I did through my dreams about something I knew hardly anything about, and to go through these adventures as a man who looks nothing like me is very convincing to me that we have all been here before.

BIBLIOGRAPHY

The following reference books have been very helpful and informative in my search for historical details of the Civil War. They have not only supplied me with the historical information I needed to corroborate the details of my dreams, they were a fascinating reading experience as well.

Arms & Equipment of the Civil War by Jack Coggins
Generals in Gray by Ezra J. Warner
Echoes of Glory: *Arms & Equipment of the Confederacy* and
Echoes of Glory: *Arms & Equipment of the Union* both by the editors of Time-Life Books
Men at Arms Series 170
American Civil War Armies & Confederate Troops by Philip Katcher and Ron Volstad
Who was Who in the Civil War by John S. Bowman
Official Price Guide to Civil War Collectibles by Richard Friz
The Tennessee Sampler by Peter Jenkins and Friends
The Life of Johnny Reb by Bell Irvin Wiley
The South by Mort Kunstler
North American Trees by Barbara Burn
The Civil War Trust's Official Guide to the Civil War Discovery Trail by Frommer
The Civil War Society Encyclopedia of the Civil War by the Philip Lief Group, Inc.

You may contact the author by writing to:

James H. Kent
24 Tappan Avenue
Trenton, NJ 08690

Please send a self-addressed stamped envelope for reply.